# AN AMERICAN CONSULAR OFFICER IN THE MIDDLE EAST IN THE JACKSONIAN ERA:

A Biography of William Brown Hodgson, 1801-1871

by

THOMAS A. BRYSON

West Georgia College

Atlanta

COPYRIGHT © 1979 BY RESURGENS PUBLICATIONS, INC. All rights reserved, including the right to reproduce the original materials in this book, or parts thereof, in any form or by any means, electronic or mechanical, including photocopying and recording, or by any information storage or retrieval system, except for the inclusion of brief quotations in a review, without first obtaining written permission from the publisher.

ISBN 0-89583-010-8
Library of Congress Catalogue Card Number: 78-78388

Manufactured in the United States of America.

Atlanta, Georgia, U.S.A.

To

the memory of my father

Thomas A. Bryson, Jr.

# PREFACE

Historians of American diplomatic history have long been concerned with the westward thrust of pioneers to fill out the continental limits of the United States and with the subsequent push across the Pacific Ocean in pursuit of the lucrative China trade. But recently, James A. Field, Jr. turned his attention to pioneers of a different variety--to the procession of American merchants, missionaries, mariners, philanthropists, educators, naval officers, and diplomats who ventured into the Middle East in ever greater numbers in the nineteenth century. Indeed, Field has noted in his monumental study, America and the Mediterranean World, 1776-1882 (1969), that Frederick Jackson Turner stood in 1893 at Cumberland Gap and looked west as American pioneers completed the settling of the frontier, a fact that gave a definite direction to the writing of American history. Field suggests that had Turner stood instead at Gibraltar looking east, he would have observed an "equally distinguished procession" of American pioneers making their way toward the Levant. Inasmuch as the Turnerians, in their obsession with the American frontier, turned their historical attention to the west, the American penetration of the Middle East, Field asserts, has been an almost forgotten saga in the annals of American history.[1] Field's work has been accompanied by studies by David H. Finnie, Joseph L. Grabill, Robert L. Daniel, L. C. Wright, A. L. Tibawi, and Roy F. Nichols.[2] Their works describe the activities and experiences of early Americans in the Middle East who were the predecessors of the oil men who arrived in the twentieth century to build an

American empire floating on a sea of petroleum. As Roy F. Nichols wrote, they were "advance agents of American destiny," so called because the American nation would one day find its industrial economy and the well-being of its people inextricably intertwined with the Arab oil-producing states.[3]

One of the early American pioneers or agents of destiny to reach the Middle East was William Brown Hodgson. Following the American Revolution, the United States, having lost access to rich markets in the British Empire, sought out new markets. The Mediterranean world proved a rich source of raw materials and a new market for American produce. Growing American commercial connections in the Middle East required that Americans have a knowledge of Middle Eastern languages, customs, diplomatic and commercial practice, and politics. So devoid of persons knowledgeable of Oriental languages was the United States, that President John Quincy Adams sent Hodgson to Algiers in 1826, there to study Turkish, Arabic, and Persian and to acquaint himself with customs and usages in the region. Hodgson's pursuit of knowledge of Middle Eastern culture, language, and diplomatic practice, and his career as an American consular officer in the Middle East from 1826 to 1842 make up the bulk of this biography. To be sure, during that period Hodgson served elsewhere but in the main his importance to history lies in his service in that distant region.

By and large, this is a critical, diplomatic biography that assesses Hodgson's strengths and weaknesses as a consular officer in the Age of Jackson, when place and position in the consular service depended upon political connections and patronage. As suggested by John A. DeNovo, I will attempt to show how the United States government sponsored Hodgson's training to enable him to serve in the Middle East.[4] I have chosen this approach because critics of the American consular and diplomatic service in the nineteenth century have pointed to the non-career-oriented nature of that service, suggesting that many of its officers were merely political appointees who obtained diplomatic posts as the spoils of office, or dilettantes--rich young sons of wealthy contributors to political parties--whose main concern was to seek broad experience in esoteric places before settling down to a life of trade, or commercial opportunists who sought posts that would enable them to derive rich economic advantages.[5] The lack of a systematic selection of candidates for the service made for rank amateurs representing the United States. But there have always been those who sought a career in the consular service, and they generally entered as a secretary of legation. Even so, the career officer needed political connections in the government. This was Hodgson's case, for he entered the service as a secretary to William Shaler, long-time U.S. Consul General at Algiers, but his retention in the service depended upon the patronage of John McLean, Postmaster General and later Associate Justice of the Supreme Court. He remained in the service until 1842 when he married a wealthy heiress and settled down to a life of scholarship, service, and ease in Savannah. This study will demonstrate that Hodgson was a career consular officer in every sense of the word and that he exhibited the professional expertise that set an example for later members of the service. He was neither a political spoilsman seeking to live off of the public largesse, nor a mere dilettante hoping to amuse himself with the study of esoteric languages, art, and customs. His professionalism makes Hodgson an exception, for critics of American diplomatic and consular officers in the Middle East indicate that the service was woefully lacking in trained personnel, many of whom were so poorly paid that they resorted to corrupt practices to supplement their meagre salaries.[6] But inasmuch as Hodgson continued to study Oriental languages after leaving the consular service, this study will also treat his activities in Savannah between 1842 and his death in 1871.

The writing of this biography was originally suggested to me by Mrs. Lilla M. Hawes, who was the director of Hodgson Hall, the Savannah headquarters of the Georgia Historical Society where Hodgson's manuscript collection is located. Mrs. Hawes made many helpful suggestions in the writing of the last two chapters of this study and improved the manuscript greatly by a critical reading of it. I am indebted to her and to her two assistants, Miss Miriam Brown and Mrs. Connie Stephenson, for their aid. I also wish to acknowledge the encouragement given me by Professors James A. Field, Jr. of Swarthmore College and John A. DeNovo of the University of Wisconsin and by Dr. Harry N. Howard, a retired Foreign Service Officer. The scholarship of these three men in American-Middle Eastern relations is well known. Professor Stanley Insler, secretary of the American Oriental Society and a member of the graduate faculty at Yale University, made several critical suggestions about Hodgson's language study. Because Hodgson's manuscript collection as related to his professional career is so limited, I have had to look elsewhere for the manuscripts to support this study. I am grateful to John McDonough, manuscripts librarian at the Library of Congress, who gave unstintingly of his time to help me locate material relative to this work. Terry Alford of the history faculty of Northern Virginia Community College gave me numerous suggestions that lead to the location of material on my subject. The staff of the American Philosophical Society made available to me the holdings of their rich archive as it related to Hodgson. I also acknowledge the assistance given me by Nicholas Biddle Wainwright and his staff at the Historical Society of Pennsylvania. Dr. Milton Gustafson, chief of the Diplomatic Branch, National Archives and Records Service, and his staff were most diligent in assisting me to locate State Department records pertinent to this work. David Trask, director of the Historical Office at the Department of State, has most kindly answered several inquiries related to my subject. I am also obliged to Lawrence Gelfand, University of Iowa, for providing me with a copy of his penetrating essay on the American diplomatic service.[7] David H. Finnie kindly supplied me with some of his notes used in the writing of <u>Pioneers East: The Early American Experience in the Middle East</u>. Adrian Colquitt, a retired Foreign Service Officer, gave me some notes that provided me with important leads in using the Hodgson papers. Professor Thomas Campbell of Florida State University read and criticized portions of the manuscript. For the able assistance given me by the library staff of West Georgia College I am most grateful. The West Georgia College faculty research council supplied me with a generous grant that sustained the research on this book. No writer is without feelings of gratitude to his family for enduring the long hours at the typewriter; my wife, Anne, and children, Tommy and Olivia, have been most understanding.

West Georgia College  Thomas A. Bryson
Carrollton

# CONTENTS

|   | Preface | vii |
|---|---|---|
| 1 | Introduction | 1 |
| 2 | Apprenticeship at Algiers | 9 |
| 3 | A Tour at the State Department | 33 |
| 4 | Service in Constantinople | 47 |
| 5 | A Secret Mission to Egypt | 83 |
| 6 | A Washington Interlude | 99 |
| 7 | American Consul at Tunis | 119 |
| 8 | Savannah and Scholarly Activities | 131 |
| 9 | Summary | 159 |
|   | Notes | 163 |
|   | Bibliography | 189 |
|   | Index | 203 |

# 1
# INTRODUCTION

Chapter 1

Introduction

Following the American Revolution, the budding American republic faced a hostile world of large empires that practiced the principle of mercantilism. American merchants and shippers found that they no longer had those trading privileges taken for granted as part of the globe-straddling British Empire. Commercial ties with France and Spain left much to be desired. Overseas commerce was a necessity for the survival of the nation. American merchants and shippers faced a depression in the Confederation Era. They decided that new markets must be found to stimulate a declining economy, and looking to the Baltic, the Orient, and the Mediterranean, they now turned their attention to these areas to compensate for trade lost with Spain, France, and Britain. American diplomacy in the Confederation Era is almost totally commercial as the nation's diplomats aided the merchant and shipper to find new avenues of trade. Yankee ships soon plied the blue waters of the Pacific between east coast ports and China and the European ports on the Baltic. But access to trade in the Mediterranean world was obstructed by the Barbary pirates of Morocco, Algiers, Tunis, and Tripoli. These predators of the Mediterranean preyed on American merchant ships in the Mediterranean, causing the commercial lobby to pressure Congress to negotiate treaties with the Barbary states. Between 1786 and 1817 the United States alternated negotiations for treaties with the employment of naval force to obtain that climate so necessary to the peaceful pursuit of trade. With the War of 1812 concluded, the U. S. Navy finally brought the obstinate Barbary pirates to bay at the mouth of a cannon. Treaties were made and Americans now freely enjoyed peaceful commerce in the Mediterranean.

The War of 1812 marked a turning point in American history. In the wake of the conflict came a tide of national fervor which left no doubt that the American republic rested on a firm foundation. This era is highlighted by optimism, confidence, individualism, and a growth of nationalism. Six new states entered the union in the years 1816-1821. But the nationalism of the era was marred by the growing sectionalism between north and south, for the questions of slavery and the tariff began to draw sharp lines of difference. But the period was also accompanied by diplomatic achievement, for in 1819 Spain surrendered Florida, and the enunciation of the Monroe Doctrine in 1823 denoted America's determination to free herself of the toils of European intrigue that she might realize her destiny in creating a continental empire between the Atlantic and the Pacific. This national spirit manifested itself in the desire to create a stronger unity, and soon the nation was crisscrossed with turnpikes, canals, and later railroad lines. In this striving for self-sufficiency, commercial men and shippers turned their hands to manufacturing. New England factories and shops were soon producing goods that competed with those made in Europe. To facilitate their economic activity, manufacturers demanded the resurrection of the United States Bank in 1816 and the passage of a high protective tariff to protect infant American industries from the English who were "dumping" their surplus goods upon American shores.

Although this period of nationalism found Americans primarily concerned with building up their nation and pursuing goals of an internal nature, there were also those that looked outward from the shores of the republic. As historian Roy Nichols wrote, there was much about the world that Americans needed to learn, and there were many tasks that they needed to perform.

Introduction    5

These included chores of a diplomatic, linguistic, commercial, missionary, and archaeological nature. The agents of America's Middle Eastern interests or destiny who performed these tasks were little known men, few of whom gained more than a footnote in history until resurrected by recent historical scholarship.[1] These men deserve their place in history, for their enterprise provided this nation with its entrée into a remote region of the world, often under the most difficult of circumstances. They gathered the information necessary to the conduct of commercial relations and diplomatic negotiations with a people long accustomed to dealing with the sophisticated Europeans who had mastered the Byzantine nature of Middle Eastern commercial and diplomatic practice. Of necessity, many of the earliest Americans to arrive in this region were members of the U.S. consular and diplomatic service. One of these men was William Brown Hodgson, the subject of this biography.

But before discussing Hodgson's entry into the consular service, a word about the nature of the American State Department is first necessary. By the middle of the nineteenth century, the only major western power that did not have a career foreign service was the United States.[2] Indeed, Robert Schulzinger asserts that the nation's career "diplomats led frivolous lives. . . ."[3] Few men chose diplomacy as a career in the early part of the nineteenth century. The typical member of the diplomatic service was a wealthy campaign contributor, a retired military or naval officer, or a political type who hoped to improve his station in life by later service in the government or by association with a corporate enterprise. Members of the consular service came from lesser ranks who depended upon family ties or political patronage for appointment. No merit system existed, and the principle of rotation in office made for insecurity of tenure. Low salaries limited the diplomatic service to men of wealth. While the consular service offered better pay, nevertheless its ranks were full of appointees who accepted a post for economic advantage or those who supplemented their meagre earnings by overcharging on consular fees and by sale of protection. To the concept of rotation in office was added the spoils system by the Jacksonians, adding further to shortness of tenure and inhibiting the professionalization of the diplomatic and consular services.[4] To make matters worse, members of the nation's consular and diplomatic service projected an image of effetism and snobbery, a condition that made a cost-conscious Congress unwilling to improve compensations and conditions necessary to the growth of a professional service.[5] What is more, the calibre of members of the service in the Middle East was low, and drunkeness and corruption were not unknown.[6]

The main avenue by which young men traveled to achieve a career in the diplomatic service was through an apprenticeship as secretary to a minister or to a consul general.[7] But opportunity was limited, for the staff of the Department of State was small during the early years of the republic. By 1820 when John Quincy Adams assumed the position of Secretary of State, the staff of the Department was fifteen, with a total outlay for salaries amounting to only $21,160.[8] Adams found the Department to be inefficient. He caused the clerks to keep an index of all correspondence for consular and diplomatic posts and for letters from foreign ministers. He also drafted a general standing instruction for all newly appointed ministers, and he was responsible for founding the State Department library.[9] On assuming the presidency in 1825, Adams continued to strive for a more professional body of men to represent the U.S. abroad. One can be sure that President Adams desired that personnel strictly adhere to the instructions that Secretary Adams had drawn up to insure a mor professional corps.[10] Thus, when Hodgson entered the consular service during Adams' administration, he embarked on his career when the nation's chief executive began to demand a degree of professionalism from the country's diplomatic and consular service. His early education suited him for this career.

Very little is known about the early life of William Brown Hodgson. He was born on 1 September 1801 in Georgetown, District of Columbia, the eldest son of Joseph and Rebecca Hodgson. His father, born in Kent

Introduction    7

County, Delaware, was a fourth generation descendant of Robert Hodgson, a Quaker clergyman who had landed in 1657 in New Amsterdam, later called New York. Persecuted for his religious views, he settled in Rhode Island. Joseph Hodgson was probably a man of modest circumstances, for his son was well known to Francis Scott Key, a Georgetown attorney and author of the "Star Spangled Banner." A memorandum in Hodgson's State Department application file indicates that Key had known Hodgson since the latter's boyhood and that he had spent much time in the Key's Georgetown home on Bridge Street.[11] Further evidence of young Hodgson's middle class status was his attendance at the classical academy in Georgetown, over which the Reverend James Carnahan, the future president of Princeton, presided between 1814 and 1823.[12] Hodgson was a diligent student of classical Greek and Latin. A copy of his academy edition of Lucian's Dialogues in Greek and Latin contains a note in his clear handwriting, "Began and finished Lucian's Dialogues in three months."[13] This was no mean task for a thirteen-year-old boy. Further evidence of Hodgson's precocious bent for language study is indicated by his exchange of letters to the editor of the National Intelligencer in April, 1821, with no less than George Watterson, Librarian to Congress. According to a note in Hodgson's manuscript collection, he engaged while still a "school boy" in a discussion on the meaning of the word "Barak." The lengthy exchange clearly indicates that young Hodgson had already developed the keenness of mind and the grasp of philology that was to enable him to make his mark in the consular service as a student of Oriental languages.[14] Hodgson did not receive a university education, for his father died while he was still young, and his mother removed the family to Richmond, Virginia. For a time Hodgson assisted his mentor at the classical academy in Georgetown, and he later received academic acknowledgement of his unusual grasp of language. In May, 1823, his former mentor was elected to the presidency of Princeton. Undoubtedly due to Carnahan's efforts, Princeton conferred upon Hodgson the honorary degree of A. M. in 1824.[15]

This was a fortunate happenstance, for in 1824 Hodgson made application to the State Department for a position as clerk-translator. His letter of application to Secretary of State John Quincy Adams carried the endorsement of Francis Scott Key and Congressman Daniel Pope Cook from Illinois. Cook's letter indicates that Hodgson had also acquired a knowledge of French and Spanish and that he was "a young gentleman of fine education."[16] Fortunately for Hodgson, John Quincy Adams was soon to become President, and he determined to employ young men in the State Department for the specific purpose of acquiring a knowledge of the Oriental languages in order to facilitate diplomatic negotiations in the Mediterranean and the Middle East where the United States had a growing commerce. What is more important, John McLean, President Adams' Postmaster General, was a personal friend of the young Virginian. McLean arranged for Hodgson to meet Adams at the White House, and, as Hodgson later wrote: "I owe my fortunes to McLean."[17] Indeed, John McLean, who would become Andrew Jackson's Postmaster General and later receive the General's appointment to the Supreme Court, provided Hodgson with the necessary connections in the executive branch of the government to remain in the consular service during the years when political patronage was so necessary.[18]

# 2
# APPRENTICESHIP AT ALGIERS

Chapter 2

Apprenticeship at Algiers

Following the exploits of Commodore Stephen Decatur's U. S. Navy squadron in 1816, peace between the Barbary corsairs and American merchantmen ensued, and there was a growing traffic between New England ports and those of the Mediterranean world. However, the United States had no trained personnel in its State Department who could converse or correspond with the peoples along the coast of North Africa, where a provincial Arabic was spoken. Due to the difficulty of obtaining translations of this language of North Africa, where commercial relations were growing, President John Quincy Adams determined to send William Brown Hodgson to Algiers, there to assist Consul General William Shaler and to perfect himself in the use of Oriental languages. It was particularly desirable that Hodgson acquire Arabic and the dialogue spoken by the local people in order that the United States might more effectively negotiate with the Barbary states. The inability to communicate with the peoples of the coast of Morocco had long been an embarrassment at the State Department, for during the administration of James Madison, letters had been received from Morocco which could not be translated.[1] Adams felt that Shaler would be the ideal mentor for Hodgson, for Shaler had served at Algiers since 1815 and during this time he had exercised his scholarly talents in a study of language and culture.[2]

Henry Clay, Adams' Secretary of State, advised William Shaler as early as 29 December 1825 of the President's intention to send Hodgson to Algiers for language training. He wrote that Hodgson had been employed at the State Department for "some time." Working as a clerk-translator, Hodgson evinced a peculiar aptitude for language study, and he had the confidence of both the President and "myself." It is anticipated, Clay wrote, that during the three years tenure at Algiers, Hodgson should perfect himself in the study of Turkish, Arabic, and the local dialect. The Secretary wrote that it was necessary to have language experts in the Department to protect the public interest, for recently a treaty had been translated in a "fraudulent interpretation."[3]

Clay wrote Hodgson on 14 January, advising that he was being posted to Algiers, there to serve under William Shaler as a language student. He noted that the President had high hopes for him. He was instructed to make periodic reports on his progress. His tenure was for three years and his salary was $600.00 per year.[4] Clay provided Hodgson with a letter of introduction to Shaler. The letter is important, for it sheds some light on Hodgson's family. Clay wrote that Hodgson was a member of a "worthy and respectable family, long resident here," and that he had personally known that family for some time.[5] Prior to his departure for Algiers, Hodgson called on President Adams, who recorded in his diary that Hodgson came to pay his respects and to express his appreciation for the opportunity to study Oriental languages. The President noted that Hodgson had a "fondness and a facility for acquiring languages quite uncommon."

Hodgson's departure from Baltimore was delayed, and he advised Daniel Brent, Chief Clerk at the Department of State, that he was using his time to study Italian and German and to acquire a collection of books on language. He sailed for Algiers on 11 February 1826 aboard the *Balloon*, a merchant ship that homeported at Baltimore.[7] Winter crossings of the Atlantic were arduous and accompanied by rough weather. Hodgson's trip was no exception. Departing Baltimore, the ship hove to off the coast of Virginia, and then started on a long, cold twenty-four day voyage to Gibraltar. Hodgson later wrote that "my sickness has been too great for humanity to endure."[8] The <u>Balloon</u> arrived at Gibraltar, and Hodgson reported to his friend Peter Force, the Washington collector and editor of historical materials, that he was "ecstatic" to be on dry land once again. Hodgson found Gibraltar interesting, for his letter to Force not only related a history of the British bastion but also gave an etymological explanation of the name "Gibraltar."[9] Departing from the British fortress the <u>Balloon</u> proceeded to Port Mahon, Minorca, where the U.S. Mediterranean squadron was anchored. Here Hodgson boarded the <u>U.S.S. Ontario</u>. She proceeded to Algiers, arriving on 12 April 1826.[10]

The city of Algiers was impressive, being located on a semicircular bay between twelve and fifteen miles wide and rising from the sea to give its occupants a commanding view of the water. It was a walled city, filled with approximately 50,000 people who inhabited small, square houses, whose whitewashed walls gleamed in the glare of the summer sun. It had narrow streets, hardly wide enough for a horse-drawn cart to pass. The houses, as is the case in the East, opened on interior courts. The city was a veritable fort, overlooked by a citadel or kasbah. At night the gates of the city were closed and the people could rest easy behind the thousand pieces of artillery mounted on the walls and citadel.[11] Of the climate, Hodgson wrote that he found it to be "salubrious, the scenery picturesque, the manner of living rather luxurious and the consular families are refined and hospitable." He observed that all of the consuls, Shaler excepted, had summer houses which served as havens from the intense heat of the summer season.[12] Shaler rented a house from the heirs of a murdered dey for $250.00 per year. It overlooked the sea, providing the occupants with a grand view of the harbor. Shaler did not fly the American flag from the house, for it was forbidden by Muslim custom. Instead, he hired a garden outside of the city and flew the flag in that small plot.[13]

Hodgson's letters to Peter Force are revealing. They indicate that Hodgson was pompous, pedantic, given to an over-weening admiration of British nobility, and somewhat self-ingratiating. Yet they also revealed him to be a man who combined an admiration of the republican principles upon which the United States was founded with a profound sense of nationalism. For example, he noted that American seamen were literate and "free men," who man the ships of the United States Navy. They were good representatives of the "American people, who sustained a character preeminent for everything that is generous and brave."[14] Yet, Hodgson's letters also indicate that he was serious about the task at hand. He wrote that Shaler was kind, had received him well, and was concerned that he progress in his language study. He observed that the Consul General had a most adequate library which would serve his needs well.[15]

If Hodgson was pleased with his mentor, the feeling was reciprocal, for Shaler advised Secretary of State Clay that he was gratified that the President had determined to send language students to the Barbary consulates to learn culture, history, and the language of the region. "W. Hodgson," Shaler wrote, "appears to possess the qualifications necessary to avail himself of these advantages, and, if I have not erred in my judgement of him, he will not disappoint the expectations of the President." He said that he appointed Hodgson as secretary to the consulate.[16] It must have been with genuine pride that Shaler, known as the "Old Consul" for his long tenure at Algiers, introduced Hodgson to the Algerian Minister of Marine at a ceremonial function that usually accompanied the arrival of a newly appointed consular official. Shaler also introduced his protégé to the members of the consular corps, several of whom became fast friends of Hodgson.[1]

It was from his friends in the consular corps that Hodgson began to acquire a knowledge of the convoluted international situation that obtained in the Mediterranean world. The Ottoman Turks had ruled Algiers since the sixteenth century. Until 1587 agents of the sultan ruled it, but after that time the sultan created separate regencies for Algiers, Tunis, and Tripoli. The Turks posted garrisons in Algiers and the other towns of Algeria, but they never extended their rule to the rural areas. In the early nineteenth century, Hussein, the Dey, ruled the Algerians. Hussein was a Turkish chief, and found it necessary to support the Turks in their effort to counter the Greeks who had begun the struggle for independence from the Ottoman overlords in 1821.[18] At the time of Hodgson's arrival in Algiers, the Algerine admiral was in command of a squadron of ships operating against the Greeks.[19] To complicate Algerian matters more, the Dey was also occupied in a war against the Spanish, and his foreign minister was engaged in communication with the British who were then trying to obtain access to the lucrative coral fishing off the Algerian coast. Internally, the Dey conducted a military expedition to put down the Kabyles, a mountain folk trying to maintain their independence.[20] Although the Algerians had abandoned piracy, Hodgson wrote Peter Force that the rebellious Kabyles had captured one American merchantman, compelling the Dey to pay the ransom for the American crew held captive.[21]

As Hodgson had applied himself to mastering the international situation in the Mediterranean, so he also applied himself to his primary duty of studying Oriental languages. William Shaler was the ideal mentor, for he had a natural bent for scholarly pursuits. Peter S. Duponceau, the noted Philadelphia attorney and officer of the American Philosophical Society, wrote Shaler in 1822, inquiring about the languages of North Africa. He was particularly interested in the Berber dialects, a subject about which scholars knew very little. Shaler applied himself to the task, studying Greek and Latin to obtain a foundation, and he soon made several reports to Duponceau which were discussed by the members of the American Philosophical Society and published in their <u>Proceedings</u>.[22] Shaler was pleased to have Hodgson at Algiers, for he wrote Duponceau that Hodgson possessed "an excellent classical" education and an "uncommon genius for philological pursuits." He noted that Hodgson's progress in the study of Arabic far exceeded his fondest expectations, suggesting that he would in time be able "to communicate interesting philological information."[23]

The "Old Consul made his library available to Hodgson, furnishing him with language books borrowed from the consular corps until others could be purchased. Hodgson advised Henry Clay that a supply of books on Arabic and Turkish had been ordered from a Paris bookshop. His initial report to the Secretary noted that he had deferred his study of Turkish until he had attained a grasp of Arabic, because study of the former presupposed a knowledge of the latter. He advised tha he had also applied himself to the Lingua Franca, a melange of the various languages spoken on the norther littoral of Africa.[24] Shaler suggested to Clay in a letter accompanying that of Hodgson, that the young language student be posted to the Levant to study Turkish, a suggestion that might have been responsible for the dispatch of Hodgson to Constantinople several years later.[25]

Unfortunately, Hodgson found it difficult to maintain his initial rapid progress in language study, for a subsequent report to Secretary Clay indicated that he experienced great difficulty obtaining the necessar Arabic and Turkish lexicons. Lack of these academic tools meant that he had "achieved but little" during the past few months. He requested permission to go to Paris, there to procure the books and obtain instruction from professors knowledgeable in the Oriental languages.[26] But Hodgson did not receive permission t go to Paris. William Shaler's health was poor, and th Department and the President found it more expedient t grant him sick leave. Hodgson expressed disappointmen in a letter to Daniel Brent at the State Department at being denied permission to visit the French capital.[27]

Hodgson informed Clay in the spring of 1827 that Sh ler had departed on the Porpoise for Port Mahon, hopin to sojourn in either France or Italy for the purpose of regaining his health. He asserted that Shaler had appointed him as Chargé d'Affaires. Hodgson advised o the increasing French hostility toward the Dey, but wrote that nothing had occurred to "disturb relations between the Algerian leader and the United States."[28]

Hodgson continued his language study, applying himself to Arabic and Turkish. Feeling confident of his ability, he began in the spring of 1827 to translate from Turkish into English. He wrote Henry Clay that he had translated the U.S.-Algerian treaty of 1816 from Turkish into English and would submit it as evidence of his growing proficiency in Turkish, the language of diplomacy in the Barbary regencies. In making his translation, he advised that he had borrowed Meninskis' <u>Arabico-Persico-Turkish Lexicon</u> from the Sardinian Consul General who employed a language student. He related that this tool greatly facilitated his work. He observed that "I speak the <u>Lingua Franca</u> with tolerable facility, from my knowledge of the Romanic /sic/ languages of which it is compounded. It is a useful medium of intercourse in these countries, being used from Constantinople to Morocco." He concluded with the news that he had spent $250.00 to purchase language books and to defray the costs for tuition in Arabic and Turkish.[29]

Hodgson confirmed the trust which Shaler placed in him. The "Old Consul" wrote Henry Clay "that you will be entirely satisfied with Mr. Hodgson; his faults are those only which naturally pertain to an ardent mind, without much experience in the affairs of men. The actual trust which I have been obliged to confide in him will fairly test his discretion, and serve as a guide to the propriety of further confidence." Hodgson is very "industrious and the progress which he has made in the study of Arabic, and even Turkish, and Persian, is beyond anything that I would have supposed possible in a single year; he translates and understands Arabic very currently; he certainly merits the patronage of the government . . . and I doubt not that he may become a very useful man and probably rank among the first philologists of his time." He concluded with the reservation that Hodgson's health was none too good.[30] But Hodgson's subsequent dispatches and reports to Henry Clay during Shaler's absence indicate that he carried out the spirit and the letter of his instructions. He duly advised Clay of Shaler's return in the autumn of 1827, saying he was expected to arrive from Port Mahon in October.[31]

But Shaler would not remain long in Algiers, for he continued to suffer with gallstones and dropsy. His sick leave at the Spanish mineral baths had done him little good, and the spring of 1828 found him ready to depart for the United States and a new assignment in the consular service. Accordingly, in March Shaler appointed Hodgson as Secretary and Chargé d'Affaires, instructing him to correspond with the Commander of the U.S. Naval squadron and the Department of State, to ascertain that the Treaty was not violated, to seek instructions from the Department should questions of a political nature arise, and "to sustain the credit of the national character in this remote region."[32] He had little to fear. In April, Shaler embarked on the *Porpoise* for the long voyage home. Putting in at Marseilles, he wrote Secretary Clay that he left Hodgson immersed in his language studies and that he had given him proper instructions to carry out the duties of Chargé.[33]

Hodgson continued to apply himself to Arabic and Turkish; and, feeling confident about his progress, he launched out into a study of Persian and modern Greek. Aware of his mentor's hopes for him, he wrote Shaler in the autumn that "I shall return home with a competent knowledge of all the Romance languages, plus German, Greek, Arabic, Turkish, and Persian." He advised that he was also involved in the study of the Berber dialect.[34]

Shaler's arrival in the United States was to Hodgson's advantage, for there the "Old Consul" wrote numerous letters on behalf of the young consular officer. He had already furthered his career by arranging for him to correspond on a regular basis with Peter S. Duponceau, the Philadelphia attorney whose interest in language matched that of Hodgson. At the suggestion of Shaler and at the invitation of Duponceau, Hodgson undertook a study of the Berber language and of the customs and traditions of the Algerines.[35] Shaler had been engaged in this study for quite some time prior to Hodgson's arrival. He advised Duponceau that he required assistance, and, at one time, the "Old Consul" considered bringing over a young child to learn to use the language. None could be found.[36] Shaler described Hodgson as "an excellent scholar of industrious habits and reputable talents." He advised Duponceau that the young man had a "singular genius for philological pursuits," and that he had become "quite familiar with the Arabic," a language in which he had acquired a vocabulary of some 2,000 words. Indicating Hodgson's religious interest, undoubtedly due to his staunch Presbyterian upbringing, Shaler related that he had analyzed the Lord's Prayer. What is more important, Shaler observed that Hodgson had begun a study of tribal life of the people of Algeria.[37]

In compliance with Duponceau's wishes, Hodgson sent him at regular intervals between 18 May 1828 and 18 October 1829 letters containing information on the Berber language and tribal customs. These letters provided students of linguistics with an early knowledge of Berber, a heretofore little-known language,[38] and early scholars of African languages noted Hodgson's contributions.[39] His initial letter, dated 18 May 1828, is important, for it demonstrates his approach to the study of Berber with the aid of a native student and his philological method. The young man forwarded to Duponceau a series of specimens of the grammar and syntax of Berber, a language spoken by the natives of North Africa at the time of the founding of Carthage. He said it had been modified by Arabic. He admitted that his knowledge of Berber was limited, but that he was assisted by a taleb or student named Hamet, who was twenty-one years old and a student of the Koran. With his knowledge of Arabic, Hodgson found it easy to communicate with Hamet, who taught him Berber via the Arabic. As for his philological study, Hodgson advised that he planned to compare the proper names of persons and places which appear in ancient history with those preserved to this day to see if there were a connection with Berber. He wrote that he hoped to show that the origin of Berber was not

Punic but had existed since early times, antedating the Phoenicians' founding of Carthage. His plan had borne fruit, for he observed that he had examined the works of Herodotus, Pliny, Strabo, Pomponius, and other Greek and Roman writers and collected a number of place names which he submitted to his taleb, who immediately recognized many of them as words of Berber. Hodgson claimed that he had met with such success that he could now hope to present proof that Berber was none other than the ancient Numidian or Libyan language.

As an example of his work, he wrote that he had examined the word <u>Atlas</u>, the name given to that chain of mountains extending from the western coast of Africa to Egypt, and found that the Berbers call it Adhraer. Further, an examination of the word <u>Thala</u>, a town celebrated in the history of the Numidian wars, was pronounced by the Kabyles, a tribe of Berbers, and written as <u>Thala</u>, meaning covered fountain. He observed that the word <u>Tunis</u>, the ancient city in Cyrenaeca, was from the Berber word <u>Thunes</u>, meaning foreigner in peace and safety. He asserted that his comparison of place names had proven disappointing, for he believed that they had "been disfigured by the Grecian and Roman writers." He did find that the name <u>Jurgurtha</u> may be easily "recognized in the Berber word <u>Jugurth</u>, signifying a crow or raven."[40]

Hodgson was fortunate in having the assistance of an educated Berber who had studied the Koran at the Theological School of Boojeiah, but what is more, William Shaler's library was at his disposal. Shaler had all of the ancient authors that Hodgson used for his philological studies and had borrowed from members of the consular corps books related to language study.[41]

That Hodgson regarded his language study as a step that would aid his career in the consular service is made evident in his next letter to Duponceau. He advised the Philadelphian that he had completed a vocabulary of some Berber words and was at work preparing a grammar as well as a translation of one of the Gospels. He said he hoped that publication of his earlier letter would aid his election into the American Philosophical Society, a reality that would abet his career.[42]

The summer of 1828 found Hodgson still at work, but the heat of Algiers must have been enervating, for his next letter to Duponceau was not written until September 1st. He advised that he continued to progress in Berber, but that he missed Shaler's association and advice. He had completed an extensive Berber vocabulary and had prepared material for the grammar. A new avenue had appeared, for Hodgson wrote that he had collected a number of Berber tales, songs, and other "specimens of that language." Obviously alluding to the heat of the city, he noted that he wished he had accompanied his taleb to his native Atlas Mountains, there to obtain a practical knowledge of the idiom. He revealed that he had found four Egyptian proper names, the etymology of which indicates Berber origins: Ammon, an Egyptian name for Jupiter, Hodgson claimed is of Libyan origin and found in the Desert of Barca where Berber is still spoken; Themis, goddess of heaven and earth, is found in the Berber to mean fire; Thebes, the capital of Upper Egypt, is a word in the Berber, meaning breast of a woman; and Thoth, the Egyptian counterpart of Hermes or Mercury, appears in Berber as a word signifying the eye. Hodgson concluded on a woeful note, saying he required a larger library to replace the books taken by Shaler at his departure.[43]

That Hodgson lacked adequate books to substantiate his studies is obvious from a letter written by William Shaler to Peter Duponceau. Shaler, having then returned to the United States, said that he had met President Adams to whom he had presented a copy of Hodgson's manuscript on the Berber language. He noted that the President gave it but a cursory glance, observing that he was satisfied with Hodgson's progress. But Shaler warned Duponceau that the essay was hastily written, incorrect in places, and was guilty "of savoring of vanity."[44] Hodgson's writing style reveals much about his personality, for it smacks of pedantry, and indicates that the young man was smitten with his own precocity. But if vanity is a flaw that frequently accompanies precocity and pedantry the handmaiden of scholarship, then it must be said that regardless of defects in his character Hodgson did make substantial contributions to learning. If his scholarship lacked the polish and finite quality that accompanies the work of the academician, it can be said that Hodgson was eager to get his work into print in order to further his career. But more will be said of his career later, for it is necessary to continue with his work on the study of the Berbers.

His next letter to the Philadelphia savant was a dissertation on the Berber tribes. He announced that he had determined that Berber was the "native idiom" of the various tribal people known as the Mozabies, Wadreagans, Wurlegans, and Kabyles. The Mozabies are white and profess the Muslim faith, while the Wadreagans and Wurlegans are black. Hodgson exclaimed, "When I first saw a Wadreagan, and heard him speak Berber, my satisfaction was as great as that of the navigator at the discovery of new land." He concluded, saying that each successive step confirms "my hypothesis that Berber is the original language of all North Africa, including the Egypts /sic/ and Abyssinia."[45]

Hodgson's interest in the tribal peoples of northern and central Africa continued, for a letter dated at Algiers, 1 June 1829, contains a lengthy description of the Fellatahs, or, Foulahs as they are known more frequently. He described them as a negroid people who, because of their warlike qualities, once dominated an extensive area of the Sudan. The great explorer Mungo Park was killed by a party of these pastoral people, who engaged in the slave trade. Hodgson's investigation of their language disclosed that their tongue was not of Arabic origin nor of the Berber. He determined that the language was simplistic, having no distinctions of gender or number and suggesting that the verbs are not inflected. His letter closed with a discussion of the geography of central Africa. Hodgson substantiated his interest in the region with a donation of $100.00, a sum to be held by Peter Duponceau, for the purpose of supporting a scientific expedition to Africa. Given the relevance of this letter to Liberia, a state then much in the news because of American interest in recolonizing slaves in this land, Duponceau sent Hodgson's letter to the American Colonization Society, and it was reprinted in the African Repository.[46]

But Hodgson's main concern was philology, and he soon returned to the study of Berber, as his later letters to Duponceau indicate. In a letter to the Philadelphian in the spring of 1829, Hodgson demonstrated that the words Osiris, Isis, Atoo, and Nile were of Berber origin. He observed that Osir carried the Berber meaning of aged, venerable man, while Isis signified daughters in the plural number. He wrote that the word Nile is of Berber origin and takes the meaning in Berber of set. It comes from the Berber Ile or Ilee. He suggested the word was changed to Nile. He added that he had conversed with the inhabitants of Dra, Tafilet, Fighig, Twat, Tegoraza, Tedeekels, Wurgelah, Ghadames, Djerbi, Gharian, and found that they all speak in Berber. His letter concluded with a few remarks about the Tuarycks, a white, Berber-speaking people who inhabit an extensive portion of the Sahara Desert, and with a grammatical sketch of the Berber language.[47]

One of Hodgson's final letters to Duponceau is most revealing, for it indicates that the former's religious interest had some depth. Under his direction, Hamet, the young Berber taleb, translated the Four Gospels and the Book of Genesis into Berber. He advised that he had been assisted by his friend Major Fraser, the British Consul at Bona, to make contact with the British and Foreign Bible Society in London.[48] In addition, he said that the Coptic language borrowed its grammatical forms from Berber. He continued his collection of words with Berber origins, saying that the words elephant, dates, ostrich, and falcon are all Berber names. He concluded, advising of his determination to continue his study of the Fellatahs.[49]

Hodgson's correspondence with Duponceau ended in the autumn of 1829, when he expressed his gratitude to the latter for encouraging him to pursue his Berber studies which he was now to lay aside. Hodgson had already written that he expected to leave for Washington at the beginning of 1830, for his three-year tour of duty would expire then. But he wrote that he hoped to continue his studies by visiting Tunis, Tripoli, Alexandria, and Cairo. Although he did not have the opportunity to travel to these Middle Eastern cities, he did receive two other compensatory honors. Duponceau, his Philadelphia benefactor, had reached the conclusion, after consultation with William Shaler, to publish several of Hodgson's letters in the Transactions of the American Philosophical Society. He advised the "Old Consul" that Hodgson's paper on the Berber language would be presented to the Society and subsequently published in the proceedings.[51] That Duponceau had placed great faith in Hodgson's scholarly ability is expressed in a letter to Henry Lee, General Jackson's appointee to replace Shaler as Consul General at Algiers. Although he had not met Hodgson, Duponceau wrote Lee that "I have satisfied myself that he is a young man of extraordinary genius, of great industry, and of sound judgement, and that he will be an honor to his country."[52] Hodgson duly thanked Duponceau for agreeing to present his paper to a meeting of the Society and for its subsequent publication in the Society's proceedings.[53] In the letter of thanks, he announced that the Royal Asiatic Society of London had elected him as a corresponding member.

Coincidental with his language studies was Hodgson's effort to collect Oriental manuscripts and books. He wrote Duponceau that "I have collected 250 manuscripts in Arabic, Turkish, Persian, and Berber." Some of them, Hodgson observed, "are precious." He said that he would like the manuscripts to remain at Washington "in accordance with my fondest desire of contributing to the glory of my country."[54] He also collected a number of books related to his studies, and he found the booksellers in Paris to be most obliging in helping him to create an "extensive Oriental library." He advised President Adams that his purchases were supported by his own funds and that his collection was extensive, given the three-year stay at Algiers.[55] Shortly after his return to the United States, Duff Green, the printer and man of affairs in Washington,

Algiers 25

published a catalogue of Hodgson's collection of Arabic, Turkish, and Persian manuscripts.[56] This collection contains two histories of the Berbers, two copies of the Koran, one of them beautifully illuminated, and no less than a dozen works of commentary on the Koran and the Muslim faith. It also contains a number of works on grammar, rhetoric, and logic.

While Hodgson's career was furthered by his endeavors in the realm of scholarship and the study of Oriental languages, what can be said of his performance as a consular officer? We have two criteria by which to measure his performance. First, there is William Shaler's letter to Hodgson, appointing him Secretary and Chargé d'Affaires in his absence.[57] He advised that his responsibilities included frequent correspondence with the naval commander of the American Mediterranean squadron, the transmission of accounts of important events to the State Department, to ascertain that the treaty with Algiers is not violated, and to "maintain the honor and dignity of this Consulate upon its actual footing." Inasmuch as Hodgson assumed the duties and responsibilities of consul, we can also apply those duties and functions of consuls listed in William Barnes and John Heath Morgan, <u>The Foreign Service of the United States</u>.[58] In addition to maintaining a letter book and other pertinent consular records, the consul was enjoined to write the Department of State, noting all incidents bearing on the commerce and navigation of the United States, to protect the rights of American citizens, and to collect information of a commercial value to the nation's commercial interests.

Of particular concern to the United States was the growing tension between Algiers and France, a turn of events stemming from French determination to enlarge a fortress for the protection of French coral interests off the coast of Algeria. During a discussion between the Dey and the French Consul, the Dey struck the latter in the face with a fan.[59] Hodgson followed the incident closely, for he advised Secretary of State Clay that France withdrew her Consul on 15 May 1827 and that on the following day the French squadron, consisting of one battleship, two frigates, one corvette, and one schooner arrived to blockade the port. The French demanded a pardon for the offense, the display of the French flag on the palace, and the firing of 101 guns in salute of the Consul. The Dey refused, promptly had the French fortress at La Cala destroyed, and sent several cruisers out with the French flag suspended from the bowsprit, a provocative act leading to the beginning of hostilities.

Hodgson described this incident as a declaration of war.[60] He kept the Department informed on the course of events, advising that the French and Algerine naval squadrons had fought an action off the coast of Algiers and that the French continued to maintain the blockade.[61] In April, 1828, he wrote that the future of the United States in Algiers would depend upon French plans which seemed to presuppose colonizing Algiers.[62] On 1 May he reported that hostilities between France and the Regency continued, but that Algiers would not seek to create difficulties for the United States. However, he wrote that he could be expected to be "harassed by petty vexations. These, it were better to disregard or skillfully to elude, for it would be difficult to imgine any advantage that could result from a controversy with Algiers." He assured the Secretary that American commerce had not suffered, but he noted that the blockade was still in force.[62]

Hodgson was correct in his assumption that U.S. relations with Algiers would depend upon French intentions, for on 14 June 1830 French forces landed in Algiers, and by 5 July 1830 the capital had surrendered. Algiers became a French colony.

The French invasion came after Hodgson had departed Algiers, but during his last two years he continued to function as Chargé d'Affaires. He reported to Secretary Clay that "I shall labor to justify His /President Adams/ confidence to maintain the honor and dignity of this Consulate upon its actual footing, and I shall carefully follow the example of Mr. Shaler." In his customary polished rhetoric, he concluded: "I shall therefore in my intercourse with this Regency, admit no innovation, nor abandon any established rule."[63] An examination of the consular records and the post papers indicates that Hodgson adhered to the letter of his instructions to maintain the letter books in order and to report frequently on the political and economic developments at his station. As was expected of him, he continued to pursue his study of Oriental languages and the culture and customs of the Berber peoples. But compliance with his instructions was not without difficulty, for he continued to experience problems sending his dispatches to the Department, frequently having to depend on French ships to transport his diplomatic pouches.[64] He recorded in the consular journal that the heat was a constant deterrent to work, and he rented a country house to escape the high temperature of Algiers during the summer. He wrote: "The withering heat of the summer forbids me to move abroad by day." He noted that the inclement weather made it difficult to carry on his studies and to perform the official duties of the consulate.[65]

In spite of the difficulties incurred at Algiers, Hodgson had determined upon a career in the consular service. During his three-year stay at Algiers, he continued a steady correspondence with those in the United States who might further his aspirations. While this might place Hodgson in the category of the political place-seeker, nevertheless, the lack of a career principle in the American diplomatic and consular service made it necessary that the career-oriented officer maintain his political fences, otherwise he might find himself unemployed. His patron was John McLean, Postmaster General in the administration of President Adams. Throughout his stay at Algiers, Hodgson maintained close touch through the mail with McLean. That he appreciated McLean's assistance is evident, but what is more apparent is his concern for the reelection of Adams to the presidency.[66] For example, Hodgson wrote that his "public career" was commenced "under the flattering auspices of your patronage, but unless I be supported by it some time longer the career once begun might come to an end."[67] Hodgson later advised McLean that he was Chargé d'Affaires in the absence of Shaler, that he had maintained the inviolability of the treaty, and that he had continued his Oriental language studies. Arabic he now read with some degree of accuracy. His study of Turkish was progressing. He lamented the great need of books to pursue his studies, but hoped to procure them from Paris. In closing, Hodgson urged McLean to apprise the President of his progress in the event that he might obtain future employment at the conclusion of his three-year tour at Algiers.[68] In a final letter written after Andrew Jackson's defeat of Adams, Hodgson wrote McLean, who would receive the General's appointment as associate justice on the Supreme Court, that he hoped to obtain the office of Oriental interpreter at the State Department. He said he had heard nothing of the new President's intentions, but that he did not wish to remain at Algiers where his health was suffering the effects of the hot climate.[69]

Hodgson deeply appreciated President Adams' assistance. He had sent him specimens of his work through the diplomatic pouches and through William Shaler who had called at the White House. In a display of vanity, Hodgson audaciously claimed that his revelations on the Berber language might well be rated with the noted Champollion's translation of the hieroglyphics on the Rosetta Stone.[70]

But Hodgson also had an advocate in William Shaler who kept up a steady barrage of letters on the young man's behalf. From Marseilles, Shaler advised Secretary of State Clay that he had left Hodgson as Chargé at Algiers where the young man was diligently pursuing his studies and was thus deserving of the respect of the President.[71] Shortly after Jackson's election in November 1828 Shaler wrote Peter Duponceau, suggesting that he commend Hodgson to General Jackson's "patronage."[72] In the following year, Shaler took the liberty of writing Martin Van Buren, General Jackson's newly appointed Secretary of State, saying that Hodgson was well along in his study of Oriental languages under the auspices of the government and that he was deserving of further consideration for employment by the new administration.[73] The "Old Consul" also wrote the Philadelphia savant, requesting that he too would write Van Buren on Hodgson's behalf, and within thirty days Duponceau advised Shaler that he had done so and had received Van Buren's assurance that Hodgson would receive favorable consideration by the new administration.[74]

Hodgson also maintained contact with the powers-that-be. He wrote Duponceau, thanking him for his intercession with the Jackson administration. He indicated that this was the first assurance that he had received of possible future employment by the Jackson administration. He advised that he had been in touch with Van Buren.[75] The "Little Magician" had been besieged with applicants for office. He advised a group of applicants that he "was indisposed to see persons who desired appointments seeking them in person at the seat of Government. . . ."[76] Thus Hodgson was employing the right approach in obtaining preferment through the efforts of McLean, Shaler, and Duponceau. But he was not idle, for he wrote Van Buren, calling attention to his study of Turkish, Arabic, Persian, and modern Greek. In closing, he wrote: "I respectfully solicit the patronage of the President in a career which I desire may be useful to my country, and which commenced under the auspices of the Hon. John McLean."[77] In a 4th of July letter to Van Buren, Hodgson struck a cord of nationalism, saying that he was diligent to maintain "the honor and dignity of this consulate." He advised that the United States continued to enjoy good repute at Algiers, where Americans were known as "men of strong sense and warlike souls. No future war can enhance the moral power which we now wield." Hodgson closed on a sad note, lamenting that he did not as yet know what the President intended to do about his future; he asserted he would continue his study of Oriental languages.[78]

Hodgson's future was soon decided after the election of Andrew Jackson in November, 1828. Jackson, prompted by Martin Van Buren, long associated with the New York political regime known as the "Albany Regency," initiated the spoils system, an expression of the belief that to the victor went the spoils of office. This new facet of American politics merely substantiated the current feeling that members of the American diplomatic and consular service should remain abroad for only three years, lest they become corrupted by the European influence.[79] In his first inaugural address Jackson asserted: "The duties of all public officers are, or at least admit of being made, so plain and simple that men of intelligence may readily qualify themselves for their performance; and I can not but believe that more is lost by the long continuance of men in office than is generally to be gained by their experience."[80] Thus Jackson added the principle of rotation in office to the American political system of appointments. To be sure, this great principle handed down to posterity by the Greeks of republican Athens does insure that office does not become the permanent property of an office-holding class. But the question might be raised: Does this principle make for a professional diplomatic and consular service? The answer to this question comes to us in the various reforms of the Foreign Service, culminating with the passage of the Rogers Act of 1924 which insured an American Foreign Service capable of competing with the professionals of Europe.

But even with the Jacksonian concepts of the spoils system and rotation in office, Hodgson would have remained at Algiers for only three years per his original appointment by Henry Clay. Too, his ill health necessitated his leaving Algiers, and he daily looked forward to the arrival of Major Henry Lee, the son of "Light Horse Harry" Lee, half-brother of Robert E. Lee, and political pamphleteer for General Jackson during the 1828 campaign.[81] Major Lee had desired the chief clerkship long held by Daniel Brent, who became Secretary of State pro tempore. Following the advice of James A. Hamilton, a close political adviser, Jackson appointed Lee to succeed Shaler as Consul General at Algiers.[82] That Lee would succeed Shaler and replace Hodgson as Chargé was known to Hodgson, who acknowledged this to Martin Van Buren, saying he hoped that the President had not overlooked the possibility of utilizing his services as an Oriental language specialist.[83]

Van Buren intended to make use of Hodgson, and on 24 July 1829 he drafted instructions ordering Hodgson to return to the United States upon the arrival of Major Lee. He advised Hodgson that the Jackson administration was satisfied with his "very laudable and commendable service" in representing the United States at Algiers. Van Buren took note of Hodgson's admirable progress in language study, and told him that the President had determined to send George F. Brown as a language student to Algiers. He wrote that Hodgson was to return to Washington immediately and that the sum of $300.00 was made available to cover his travel expenses.[84]

Major Lee, accompanied by his wife and George F. Brown, arrived at Algiers on 2 October on board the U.S.S. Ontario. Hodgson formally presented the Major to the Minister of Marine, who directed foreign affairs for the Dey, and to the Dey. To his delight Hodgson learned that the latter dignitary was pleased with his performance because he had shown "respect and civility" toward the Regency. Having taken care to deliver to Major Lee the records of the consulate, Hodgson departed Algiers on 9 October on board the Ontario, bound for Barcelona. From there he proceeded overland to Paris, there to purchase some Oriental books and manuscripts and to make the acquaintance of some professors of Oriental literature. At Paris he wrote Secretary Van Buren, thanking him for permission to visit the French capital on his return trip. He also praised the decision to send George F. Brown to Algiers to study foreign languages.[85]

Hodgson took his leave of the French capital in late November and took ship from the port of La Havre on 1 December, arriving in New York City on 8 January 1830. He advised his old mentor William Shaler of his crossing and of his visit to Paris, where he purchased books valued at $400.00. He bemoaned the fact that he could not visit England, but said he had hastened home to see that his career held some future. He informed Shaler that he was most happy to return to the United States, but that he would be willing to return abroad to another post in "pursuit of my ambition." Hodgson's ambition would soon be gratified with an appointment to the Department of State.

# 3
# TOUR AT THE STATE DEPARTMENT

Chapter 3

A Tour at the State Department

Hodgson arrived in New York City on 8 January. Since his letters do not reflect a bout with seasickness, we can assume that the crossing was none too rough and that he spent an interesting time studying his recently acquired store of books on Oriental languages. From New York he journeyed to Philadelphia, where he wrote William Shaler on 12 January, advising that he had visited Peter S. Duponceau. He related that Duponceau had received him cordially and had invited him to dinner and then taken him to a musical party that evening. Duponceau had given him the galley proofs of his article which was to appear in the <u>Transactions of the American Philosophical Society</u>. A few corrections were necessary to put the work in good order.[1]

It must have been a happy Hodgson who traveled down to Washington. Contemplating his future publication and anticipating future employment at the State Department, he wrote from the nation's capital to Shaler, the newly appointed Consul General at Havana, saying that he had visited President Jackson and Secretary of State Van Buren. Both men had received him well, and Van Buren had invited him to dinner. Hodgson cautioned that Major Lee's nomination had not yet been acted upon by the Senate. He closed with a brief discussion of his handling of Shaler's private affairs in Algiers and of his introduction of Major Lee to the Minister of Marine, the Dey, and the consular corps of Algiers.[2]

Hodgson was fortunate in having William Shaler to intercede with Van Buren for him, for the "Old Consul" had long had good relations with the "Little Magician." Hodgson's friend John McLean did not enjoy favor with Van Buren, whose word in matters of patronage was supreme at the State Department.[3] The newly-appointed Secretary removed eighteen of twenty-six clerks at the Department, an indication of his firm belief in the spoils system, which he was responsible for introducing to Washington as a legacy from the Albany Regency.[4] But despite McLean's lack of power with Van Buren, Hodgson did now have a good relationship with the Secretary. McLean was then safely ensconsed as an associate justice of the Supreme Court.

Since Hodgson was not immediately employed, he found time on his hands to make visits to old friends and to see something of the city of Washington. On 16 January he called on President John Quincy Adams, then residing at Meridian Hill, the Washington home of Commodore David Porter. Adams' <u>Diary</u> indicates that the former President thought highly of Hodgson. He wrote: "He had an extraordinary facility at learning languages and had already made some progress in the Hebrew, Arabic, and Persian, and we in this country were so destitute of persons versed in the Oriental languages that we could not even procure a translation of any paper which occasionally came to us in Arabic." Adams related that Hodgson had called upon President Jackson and Van Buren, but was not yet sure of future employment. He noted that the young linguist had procured a valuable collection of manuscripts and books which he hoped to sell to the Department. Adams advised Hodgson to see Daniel Brent about the matter of the sale.[5]

Although Hodgson's professional career had begun during the administration of President Adams, his fortunes were to continue during Jackson's tenure in the White House. Hodgson wrote Shaler in late February that a bill had passed both houses of Congress creating for him the office of Translator of Foreign Languages and Oriental Interpreter. He said the office carried a salary of $1,000.00 per year, with a promise that it might be increased by $350.00. He stated that Judge McLean advised him not to take the position, but he said he accepted it gladly, for he had the opinion that he would probably be sent to Constantinople as Secretary-Interpreter during the next year. Hodgson gleefully told the "Old Consul" that he had the best wishes of the Jackson administration, for Van Buren had told him that if Congress had not provided a position for him that he (Van Buren) would have found something for him. He boasted that he had dined with the President and Van Buren, attended numerous parties, and was appalled by the political intrigue in the capital. He related that he found it somewhat "humiliating to be here and find myself in the rear, when for four years, I ranked par inter pares." He apprised Shaler of the fact that the applications for the Barbary consulates are "countless," adding that the Senate had not yet acted on Major Lee's nomination to the consulate at Algiers and that a mutual friend told him that Lee would not be confirmed. He lamented that his work on philology must be deferred for a while, but that Mr. Duponceau corresponded with him regularly. Although Washington provided a favorable atmosphere for his literary pursuits, he advised that he did not like the city because of its "cold, hollow, unreal character. I prefer to live in Barbary, or anywhere out of Washington," Hodgson confided to Shaler.[6]

The city of Washington was indeed not much to brag about in 1830. Although Hodgson was staying at Gadsby's Hotel, the most popular hostelry in town, the city bore a greater resemblance to a large village than to a national capital. The city streets were dusty in summer and a veritable morass during the wet, winter months. There were then few houses on Capitol Hill, and only Pennsylvania Avenue, between the Capitol and the White House, was paved. Interspersed between the Capitol and the White House were a few houses and numerous pastures, with flocks of cattle idly grazing. At the four corners of the White House stood the plain brick buildings occupied by the personnel of the departments of State, War, Treasury, and Navy. West of the White House were more pastures and enclosed fields, and Massachusetts Avenue was out in the country. Diplomats and people of fashion lived in Georgetown in the 1830s. This quaint city had narrow, well lighted streets, with many imposing houses. Ships continued to dock at Georgetown. Aside from the Capitol and the White House, there were no buildings of architectural note in Washington. The State Department, where Hodgson performed his tasks, was a plain brick building, with a museum of portraits of Indian chiefs who had visited Washington. The Capitol was unfinished, but a visit to the Senate would have revealed a coterie of illustrious men such as John C. Calhoun, Daniel Webster, Henry Clay, Thomas Hart Benton, John Forsyth, and others. The White House was imposing, for the large pillars of the ballustrade had been completed, and the grounds had been landscaped. In those early years, few families had permanent residences in Washington, for most politicians rented houses, which could be had for from $50.00 to $300.00 per year, or else stayed in one of the numerous boarding houses. The population of the nation's capital was a modest 20,000. Entertainment was rough and ready, for horseracing, cockfighting, and heavy drinking were the order of the day. Despite its spartan physical appearance, Washington put on quite a social season when Congress was in session. Many parties were given, and leaders of fashion imitated the latest styles of Paris and London. While the Jacksonian era is noted for its association with the common man, nevertheless the social occasions of the time were gala. Social leaders were Mrs. Edward Livingston, Mrs. Andrew Stevenson, Mrs. Louis McLane, and Mrs. John Forsyth. Society, like politics, split along lines of power. Men attended parties where the city's social belles could be attired in high fashion, only to retire to smoke-filled rooms to fight for place and prestige, while their wives struggled for social leadership.[7]

In 1830 Washington was a hotbed of political contention, for already the forces of Calhoun and Jackson were on the field of battle in the Senate, where the famous Hayne-Webster debate was taking place. Hodgson's letter of 20 February 1830 spoke of the political intrigue, but in a tone of understatement. Hodgson was adept in stepping from one faction to another. He had found place during the Adams administration and had enjoyed the friendship and patronage of John McLean. McLean by 1830 was a Calhoun man, and, desiring not to remain in Jackson's cabinet, had obtained an appointment to the Supreme Court. Hodgson had been a friend of Peter Force, who now published the Washington *National Journal*, an anti-Jackson, pro-Adams newspaper. Hodgson was also on good terms with Duff Green, the publisher of the *United States Telegraph*, a Jackson newspaper. But Green later sided with Calhoun, and Jackson dumped him and turned to Francis Blair, who founded the pro-Jackson *Washington Globe*.[8]

Even though he found himself enmeshed in the political coils of Washington during a time when party battles reached epoch-making proportions and found himself engaged in his work at the Department of State, where he had little time for scholarship, nevertheless Hodgson did keep his hand busy in language study. In 1830, Duff Green, the publisher who was soon to go over to the forces opposed to Jackson, published for the young scholar *A Catalogue of Arabic, Turkish and Persian Manuscripts: The Private Collection of Wm. B. Hodgson*.[9] This collection included those manuscripts that Hodgson had purchased during his stay in the Middle East and on his trip through Paris in 1829. They were later sold to the British Museum in 1833.[10] An additional honor came Hodgson's way when in January, 1830, he was elected a Foreign Member of the Royal Asiatic Society of London.[11] In that same month Peter S. Duponceau and John Vaughn proposed Hodgson for membership in the American Philosophical Society. Their letter of introduction and endorsement showed Hodgson to have good credentials, including membership in the Royal Asiatic Society and the publication of philological and historical communications.[12] Hodgson's letter acknowledging membership in the Society, advised that he would continue to contribute to the "object of the Society--the promotion of useful knowledge."[13] Although Hodgson proposed to the American Philosophical Society that he would continue to contribute to the Transactions of the Society, he was not above making a profit on his work. In May 1830, William Shaler paid a visit to John Quincy Adams, asking the former President if he thought it proper for Hodgson to sell to the British and Foreign Bible Society his manuscript translation of the Book of Genesis and three of the Gospels which he had caused to be written in Berber. Adams replied in the negative, saying that an employee of the Department of State should receive no recompense from any foreign individual or society, except with the approbation of the President and the Secretary of State.[14] Hodgson obviously conferred with Shaler prior to his departure for his post in Havana. He also obtained the requisite permission of President Jackson and Secretary Van Buren, for in 1831 he sold the Book of Genesis and the Four Gospels to the British and Foreign Bible Society for the sum of one hundred and fifty pounds. From this collection, the Society eventually published twelve chapters of the Book of Luke, thus publishing the first sample of Berber to be printed.[15] Finally, Hodgson took an interest in the American Colonization Society, founded in 1817 to solve the problem of slavery in America. Not only was notice made of his writings in Algiers in the Colonization Society's African Repository, but the Society's files contain a letter from Hodgson to R.R. Gurley, secretary of the Society, advising that he would send him an approximate version of the writings of Abd es-Rahman, an Arabic-writing slave.[16]

But Hodgson's scholarly pursuits were deferred during his time in Washington, for affairs at the Department of State consumed most of his time. I have been unable to determine the extent of his work, but he presumably served as a clerk-interpreter. The number of clerks in the Department of State expanded at this time, and undoubtedly Hodgson was permitted to give his talent for languages full range. The United States was then engaged in the negotiation of a Treaty of Amity and Commerce with Turkey, and no doubt communications from the Sublime Porte to the Department of State required Hodgson's attention.

While it is true that the Jacksonians looked to the West where the question of Texas was looming larger in the prospects of the United States, they were also interested in foreign trade. In 1829 the United States obtained a Treaty of Amity and Commerce with Austria, and in the following year an Anglo-American agreement was struck whereby Yankee merchants could enjoy direct trade with the British West Indies. Finally, in May 1830 the United States obtained a long-sought Treaty of Amity and Commerce with Turkey.[18] Since Hodgson would soon travel to Constantinople with the ratified copy of the Turco-American Treaty to exchange ratifications with the Turks, a word needs to be said about the background to that treaty.

So important was the negotiation of a treaty with Turkey that Martin Van Buren recorded that it was the first negotiation undertaken by the Jackson administration. Apprehensive lest other powers might interfere with the negotiations in a manner prejudicial to the United States, Van Buren retained in his possession all of the papers germaine to the diplomatic intercourse.[19] A study of these papers would have revealed to the Secretary that from the years immediately following the Revolution when the United States ceased to enjoy commercial privileges as a member of the British Empire, American policy-makers had attempted to increase trade with Turkey. But American commerce with the Turks grew slowly due to the obstruction of the Barbary pirates. Nevertheless, this trade increased when the Barbary corsairs were routed, and the number of American merchantmen in the Turkish port of Smyrna grew in number. But they were at a disadvantage because of the absence of treaty relations with the Ottoman Empire. It is true they were allowed to share privileges of the Levant Company, the holder of a monopoly of British trade in the Middle East, but they were compelled to pay a tariff applicable to the British, plus an extra fee to the British consul.[20] Between 1800, when Captain William Bainbridge carried an Algerian ambassador and tribute to Constantinople and learned of the Sultan's wish to negotiate a treaty with the United States, and 1830 when the treaty was finally concluded, there occurred more than a generation of frustrated efforts to negotiate a treaty with the Turks. International complications stemming from the war between France and Spain during the Napoleonic era, the Barbary factor, the War of 1812, the Greek Revolution, and the machinations of the European Powers provided insuperable barriers to the conclusion of a Turco-American treaty of commerce. Although an American merchant, David Offley, was able to induce the Sultan to grant the United States a kind of private, most-favored-nation treaty awarding Yankee merchants and shippers commercial equality, there was no treaty to guarantee the continuation of this status for a growing American commerce.[21]

American trade with the Turks increased, for Yankee sailors carried opium from Smyrna to China, and they sold rum to the Turks in exchange for nuts, hides, figs, wool, and silver. The number of American ships at Smyrna grew in number between 1801 and 1812, when the War of 1812 intervened. Following the war some thirteen American ships on the average visited Smyrna, with a total value of cargoes at one million dollars. That number would rise to forty-six in 1832, placing the United States second only to Great Britain in the Turkish trade.[22] This growing trade made it imperative that the United States protect its interest with a commercial treaty.

While Federalist merchants from Boston had pressured Congress for many years for a treaty, it was ironically the administration of President Andrew Jackson, that uncommon son of the frontier who represented the aspirations of the common man, who finally secured a treaty. During much of the Jacksonian era there was a great boom in the United States. In the 1830s American ships plied the waters of the seven seas, reaching a position second only to that of Great

Britain in the world's carrying trade. Jackson sent out agents to the Far East in search of new avenues of commerce. They sought additional outlets in Latin America and in Europe. The growing American navy was a testimony to the enhanced commercial status and political prestige of the American republic.[23]

That the United States had the capacity to build a larger navy and merchant marine was a most important factor in deciding the Turks to negotiate a commercial treaty with the United States. The Sultan's fleet had suffered a disastrous defeat at the hands of the European Powers at the Battle of Navarino on 20 October 1827, requiring that he find new ships for his sadly depleted navy. It was the desire for Yankee, fir-built frigates that determined the Sublime Porte to make a treaty with the United States.[24]

The growing American commerce with Turkey, coupled with the Sultan's need for American ships to replace his losses, created the auspicious circumstances for the completion of a treaty. President Jackson appointed in September 1829 Captain James Biddle, U.S. Navy, David Offley, and Charles Rhind, a merchant, as commissioners to negotiate the treaty. The three men proceeded to Smyrna from Port Mahon, and then Rhind went on to Constantinople, and there on 7 May 1830 he successfully negotiated a treaty with the Sublime Porte. This agreement provided most-favored-nation treatment on the tariff, the right of extraterritoriality, and it also included a secret article requiring the American minister to help the Turks to make shipbuilding contracts in the United States and to procure ship timber.[25]

Rhind's signing the treaty miffed Offley and Biddle who grew increasingly disillusioned with the secret article. That the United States would agree to assist the Sultan in the building of a navy and the procurement of ship timber seemed to them a violation of the principle of noninvolvement, as indeed it was. The Senate approved on 2 February 1831 the public articles of the treaty, but it rejected outright the secret article. Opponents claimed that it might well enmesh the country with foreign nations in violation of the Monroe Doctrine.[26]

Senate rejection of the secret article dismayed Charles Rhind, who hoped to return to Turkey with the ratification of the treaty. His plan called for Henry Eckford, a shipbuilder who had made a name for himself during the War of 1812 and had designed the Robert Fulton, to sail to Constantinople, carrying with himself the ratified treaty. On arrival at the Turkish capital, Rhind hoped to exchange ratifications with the Sublime Porte to whom he would be accredited as the new American minister resident. Then he would be able to utilize the services of Eckford to achieve the purpose of the secret article.[27] But this was not to be, for the President appointed Commodore David Porter as the American Chargé d'Affaires, and he designated William Brown Hodgson rather than Rhind to take the treaty to Constantinople. The President passed over Rhind because of his involvement in the sale of four Arabian horses which the Sultan had presented him on the signing of the treaty.

The matter of the Arabian horses which led to Hodgson's appointment needs a word of explanation. The Sultan had given Rhind the four horses for having negotiated the treaty. Rhind claimed to have a right to the horses which he brought to New York City. Jackson wrote James H. Hamilton, U.S. District Attorney in the Southern District of New York that Rhind had caused him "much pain" because he had assumed that he could retain possession of the animals. He noted that he hoped Rhind would surrender title to the horses and take the ratified treaty to Commodore Porter at Port Mahon. Hamilton wrote Jackson on 9 April 1831, asserting that Rhind's conduct in the matter precludes his being employed, and "I think it would be well to send Mr. Hodgson forthwith to Porter with the Treaty." Jackson replied to Hamilton on 12 April, saying that the John Adams would sail in a few days from Norfolk for Port Mahon, and that he had determined to send Hodgson to transmit the papers to the Commodore. Further, that he had decided that the U.S.

Marshal in New York should sell the horses for the United States Government. The horses were sold pursuant to the U.S. Constitution which forbade any public official from receiving gifts from foreign governments, and so it might be said that Hodgson continued to pursue his career in the Middle East on the backs of four Arabian horses.[28]

# 4
# SERVICE IN CONSTANTINOPLE

Chapter 4


Service in Constantinople


On 15 April 1831 Secretary of State Martin Van Buren ordered Hodgson to proceed to Norfolk, there to take passage on the U.S.S. John Adams, due to leave shortly for the Mediterranean. Hodgson learned that he was to carry dispatches to Port Mahon where he was to place them in the hands of Commodore David Porter, the newly appointed American Chargé d'Affaires to Constantinople. Hodgson was to proceed in company with Porter to Constantinople, participate in the exchange of ratifications of the Turco-American Treaty, and then return to the United States with the ratification. In the event that Porter declined to accept the post as Chargé, Hodgson was instructed to open the dispatches to Porter, execute the exchange of ratifications, and return to the United States. Hodgson was provided with a letter of credit in the amount of $25,000.00 for the purchase of presents to be given at the time of the exchange.[1] In addition, Hodgson was the bearer of three letters: the first, was from President Jackson to the Sultan, advising that Hodgson or Porter would effect the exchange of ratification, and that either would explain the Senate's rejection of the secret article; the second, was from Martin Van Buren to the Reis Effendi or Turkish Foreign Minister, notifying him that Commodore Porter was the newly appointed American Chargé; and the third,

was a letter of credence from Van Buren to the Reis
Effendi, advising that Hodgson was empowered to exchange the ratification in accordance with the attached power of attorney signed by President Jackson in the event of Porter's refusal to accept the office of Chargé.[2]

Hodgson must have been overjoyed to be employed to return to the Middle East, for his letter to Judge McLean carried a note of enthusiasm. Announcing his departure for Norfolk on 22 April, Hodgson explained the nature of his mission to his patron. He concluded with the hope that he would return to Washington in December and there find that the President had appointed him to a position with the American Legation in the Ottoman capital.[3]

Hodgson duly repaired to Norfolk, but on learning of a delayed sailing, he paid a last minute visit to his family at Richmond. Following a short stay at his home, Hodgson sailed from Hampton Roads on 4 May. His letter to the Secretary of State indicated that he expected to arrive at Constantinople on or about 4 July, thus involving him in a two month ocean journey.[4] Given the conditions of ocean travel in the early 19th century Hodgson must have sailed with a degree of trepidation. An account of a cruise by the U.S.S. Delaware to the Mediterranean during the years 1833, 1834, and 1835 shows thirty-seven deaths, the majority attributed to cholera or consumption.[5] But had Hodgson known that his relations with Commodore Porter would eventually become as storm-tossed as the Atlantic in winter, he would have had even greater trepidation.

Commodore David Porter was both a hero and a man living under a cloud. After a long, distinguished naval career that included service aboard the ill-fated Philadelphia and a noteworthy cruise aboard the Essex during the War of 1812, Porter found lady luck turning very rapidly against him. After a most successful cruise in the Caribbean Sea to put down piracy, Porter was court-martialed for hostile acts against a friendly power. He resigned from the U. S. Navy, served for a time in the Mexican Navy, and then his fortune turned when General Jackson entered the White House. Jackson offered his old friend a captaincy in the Navy which Porter rejected outright. The General then appointed him Consul General at Algiers to replace Major Lee who had been rejected by the Senate. Following the French takeover, which made his appointment redundant, Jackson appointed Porter as American Chargé at Constantinople.[6]

The Commodore awaited Hodgson's arrival at Port Mahon, which the John Adams reached on 11 June. Hodgson duly delivered Porter his orders appointing him as Chargé, but he advised Secretary of State Edward Livingston, Van Buren's successor, that he would return the documents empowering him to exchange the ratification in the event Porter refused the post.[7] Porter accepted the position and informed the Secretary that he and Hodgson would proceed jointly to Constantinople via Naples, where they would make a brief stop to procure presents for the officials of the Sultan.[8] The two men shared a cabin aboard the John Adams, and Hodgson must have found this an interesting experience. At first blush he probably found the former naval person to be an acceptable companion. David H. Finnie described Porter as "small, dark, weather-beaten, much broken in health, and remarkably mild and quiet in his manners."[9] Porter and Hodgson, who would become inveterate enemies, undoubtedly had an amicable voyage, for their communications to the Secretary reflect no discontent. The John Adams arrived at Naples on 11 July, but the two men made no purchases, for they agreed that the presents could be bought more reasonably at Constantinople.[10] Sailing from Naples on 12 July, the John Adams, accompanied by Henry Eckford's sailing ship, brought Porter and Hodgson to Smyrna on the 24th, and following a brief stay they proceeded on to Constantinople.

The voyage from Smyrna to the Ottoman capital was a notable one, for the John Adams did not arrive until 9 August. The delay was brought about by an episode that brings out a flaw in the character of Commodore Porter that would have ominous consequences for Hodgson in due time. By long custom the Turks required all ships passing through the Dardanelles to procure a permit or firman and, if a warship, to dismount its guns. Porter, displaying a stiff-necked attitude, refused to permit Captain Vorhees to dismantle the guns of the John Adams.[11] This resulted in a delay in the American vessel moving through the Straits to the Turkish capital. Ultimately, a firman arrived, and the ship proceeded to Constantinople, where Porter perpetrated another episode. As the John Adams and Henry Eckford's ship arrived off the Seraglio Point adjacent to Constantinople, Porter demanded that the Turks render the proper salutes. This too violated custom, for the Turks gave no salutes and expected none. By his obstinate attitude, Porter created a cause célèbre in the Frankish community in the Turkish capital.[12] Porter's quarterdeck attitude, acquired from long years commanding a ship of the line, reflected a deep-seated character fault that would later cause him difficulty with his subordinates.

Porter and Hodgson arrived at Constantinople on an inauspicious note, but they immediately went to pay their respects to the Capudan Pacha, the commander of the Turkish navy, in order to smooth over the hard feelings caused by the incidents surrounding the passage of the Straits and the matter of the exchange of salutes. But the arrival was also ill-omened for another reason. There had occurred a terrible fire in the district of Pera, where European diplomatic officials and commercial representatives were accustomed to reside. The fire was accompanied by an outbreak of the plague and a widespread incidence of cholera.[13] For this reason, Commodore Porter settled at Byukdere, about nine miles above Constantinople on the Bosporus and some four to five miles from the Black Sea. This would place Porter and Hodgson at an inconvenience, for they were at some distance from the Sublime Porte and from the district where the banks, shipping representatives, and other European commercial agents were located. The city of Constantinople is in reality a collection of three towns, Stamboul, Galeta-Pera, and Skutari, in addition to a number of suburbs spread for some distance on both sides of the Bosporus. Stamboul and Pera are located on the European shore, separated by the Golden Horn, an inlet on the Bosporus. Skutari is located on the Asiatic shore, making Constantinople the only city in the world that is located on two continents, Asia and Europe. Although Porter and Hodgson elected to reside in the resort of Byukdere, they did enjoy certain advantages there. It was a Christian community, composed chiefly of the palaces of the ambassadors of the European dignitaries and of their attachés. The Commodore chose to rent a house for the sum of $250.00 per year, and, as was the custom with other diplomatic agents, he posted two guards attired in full ancient costume at the gate.[14] At the approach of a diplomatic person, the guards would strike a bell, giving three strokes for an ambassador, two for a minister, and one for a chargé. Communication was by a kaick, a long narrow light boat like an Indian canoe, with each end turned up and highly ornamented with carved work and gilding. A man's rank was known not only by the number of bells he received, but also by the number of oars in his kaick. This protocol must have seemed fitting and proper to the Commodore, who recorded interesting comments in his letters to a New York gentleman about the city of Constantinople.[15] It would also have struck Hodgson's fancy, for he too was impressed by the protocol that accompanied the work of diplomatic agents.

To a man of the Commodore's temperament, one long accustomed to having his every order issued from the quarterdeck obeyed immediately, the delay in achieving the exchange of ratifications with the Turks must have been frustrating. He advised Secretary of State Livingston that Nicholas Navoni, the dragoman attached to the American Legation, had waited on the Reis Effendi, who declared that the Sublime Porte would not receive any representative of the United States with the title of Chargé d'Affaires, because by custom the Porte only received ministers and ambassadors.[16] But the rejection of the secret article presented a problem, and Charles O. Paullin claimed that the Turks raised numerous objections to the Senate's failure to approve this feature of the treaty.[17] Indeed, Porter apprised Livingston that an agent of the Capudan Pacha was then at Smyrna, bound for the United States to purchase timber and naval stores in accordance with the secret article. The Commodore stated that he would set forth the American reasons for rejection. He did note that Eckford's presence in Constantinople was salutary, for the shipbuilder would be able to construct ships for the Sultan's navy.[18] Protocol and the question of the secret article aside, Stanley Lane-Poole suggests that negotiations at Constantinople, whether open or secret, did not move expeditiously, and more often than not months were consumed in the process of consumating diplomatic ends.[19]

Hodgson must have found the delay equally frustrating, for his career in the State Department was not yet assured, and the young Virginian desired to return to Washington, there to ascertain his professional future. Hodgson observed that protocol was at the bottom of the delay, suggesting that the Turks did not customarily treat with any diplomatic agent lower than a minister. However, he suggested that Nicholas Navoni seems to have hoped that Porter would tire of the devious ways of the Turks, depart the scene, and leave Navoni in charge of American affairs. He informed Livingston that he had held conversations with the Reis Effendi, with a view to speeding up the exchange. The talks, Hodgson noted, were held in Turkish, and he said that the Reis Effendi had assured him that an audience would be forthcoming.[20] Hodgson's letter reveals a note of anxiety, and one can assume that he desired to return to the United States with the ratified treaty as soon as possible, in order to look to his future. But Hodgson did not have too much to fear on this question, for Commodore Porter wrote the Secretary of State, declaring that Hodgson was at the Reis Effendi to attend to the translation of a portion of the treaty. He related that Hodgson's service had been "incalculable." He expressed the view that the corps of professional dragomen in Constantinople are of poor quality, an estimate repeated in his collection of published letters, and he confided that it was his intention to get rid of Navoni, whom he distrusted. He urged that "the government could not dispose of the position any better than by giving the post of dragoman to Hodgson."[21]

A word needs to be said here about Hodgson's possibilities as the American dragoman and about the role of Navoni. At this stage of his development, it is questionable that Hodgson possessed a sufficient grasp of Turkish to act as First Dragoman. This view is substantiated in David Hunter Miller's commentary on the U.S.-Turkish Treaty,[22] and by Hodgson's letters to the Department from Algiers, advising that his study of Arabic must precede that of his study of Turkish. Whatever his talents, Hodgson simply would not have had the time or the requisite conversational practice to perfect his use of Turkish. Even so, the Commodore seems to have been justified in suggesting that Hodgson replace Navoni. Although the Italian's friends claim that Hodgson schemed to have Navoni removed that he might obtain the post,[23] there is considerable evidence to show that Navoni was not a man of good character. Navoni had been dismissed by the British and Neapolitan embassies and his private life left much to be desired.[24] At all events, the Commodore had determined to retain Hodgson to assist him in the exchange of ratifications and had given him a strong recommendation for the post of dragoman.

Ultimately, the Sultan agreed to exchange the treaty ratifications, and on 5 October 1831, Commodore Porter, escorted by Hodgson, Mr. Ascaroglou, an interpreter, and a Turkish guard, started up the Bosporus in a six-oared kaick. Porter carried the treaty and presents worth about thirty thousand dollars. About half way to the residence of the Reis Effendi, the party was caught in a hail storm. One of the three oarsmen had his hand smashed, while Hodgson received a severe blow on the leg, and the Commodore was struck on the right hand. Balls of ice as large as a doubled fist struck the water about the frail craft. One of them hit the blade of an oar and split it neatly.[25] Thoroughly drenched, the party arrived for the exchange. There seems to be some difference of opinion about the event. Porter's nephew, David Dixon Porter, and Archibald Turnbull would have us believe that the exchange took place in the presence of the Sultan at the imperial palace.[26] But Porter's own description must serve as best evidence. The Commodore relates that the exchange took place in the house of the Reis Effendi, which he described as an "ordinary old red wooden house, so near the water in the village of Candalie as to step from the boat into his door." The exchange did not then take place in the midst of oriental splendor in the presence of the Sultan and all of his imperial officers. The minister, accompanied by his dragoman and attended by six servants, met the Commodore who was accompanied by Hodgson and Ascaroglou. Following a greeting, Porter and his party were entertained with the customary pipes, coffee, and sherbert. Porter then presented the gifts for the Sultan: a snuff-box worth about $9,000.00 and a fan worth approximately $5,000.00. The other presents consisted of ornamented snuff-boxes of a value in porportion to the rank of the recipient. The ceremony of exchange followed, with the Reis Effendi and Porter rising, lifting the treaties head high and making the exchange in the same motion. Porter turned the ratified treaty over to Hodgson for safe-keeping. The Turkish treaty was inscribed on thick vellum paper and contained an endorsement in Turkish. The party then smoked another pipe, accepted more coffee and sherbert, engaged in conversation about life in the United States, and then departed. Since the Commodore made no further comment about the storm, we can assume that the return trip was much less eventful.[27] Inasmuch as Charles O. Paullin and David Finnie relied on the Commodore's description of the ceremony rather than that of the Commodore's nephew or Turnbull, we can assume that the latter two were inaccurate and much embellished.[28]

Hodgson was undoubtedly relieved to have the ceremony concluded and to feel free to return to Washington with the ratified treaty and to look into the possibilities of his future employment. At this point, the young Virginian had the full confidence of Commodore Porter, who reported to Secretary Livingston that he had experienced "immense advantages from the assistance of Mr. Hodgson." Continuing, Porter acknowledged that "I should have found it extremely difficult to have brought matters to a satisfactory conclusion without his services." He affirmed that "It is my sincere hope that the government will attach him to the mission as its interpreter, to do the duties of Secretary of Legation." He concluded with the news that Hodgson was returning the ratified treaty to the United States.[29]

But Hodgson had not been idle in the matter of furthering his career. An examination of his application file in the Department of State records reveals that the young Virginian had first applied to Martin Van Buren for the post of First Dragoman at the American Legation which would open in Constantinople.[30] Arriving at Port Mahon en route to Constantinople, he learned that Edward Livingston had succeeded Van Buren, and he promptly wrote the new secretary that he wanted to apply for the post of dragoman. Failing to receive this post, Hodgson declared he would like a post "in the foreign service where my Oriental acquisitions may be rendered useful to my Government and my country."[31] From Constantinople he wrote Livingston, observing that the Commodore had suspended Navoni and that he would like to renew his application for the post of First Dragoman.[32] Hodgson's application carried three very influential endorsements. Andrew Stevenson, Speaker of the House of Representatives, wrote that the appointment would give him "much pleasure."[33] Peter S. Duponceau wrote two letters, affirming that he took pride in having first introduced Hodgson to the administration of General Jackson and that he felt the applicant was fully qualified for the position.[34] James Carnahan, then president of Princeton, wrote that Hodgson had been his pupil in a classical school at Georgetown where he subsequently acted as the master's assistant. He lauded Hodgson, maintaining he had never known a person with greater "aptitude in the acquisition of languages."[35]

With the strong recommendation of Porter, Hodgson departed Constantinople on 9 October, reassured about his future status in the consular service. He stopped off at the port of Smyrna and visited David Offley, the American consul at Smyrna who had been a member of the commission appointed to treat with Turkey in 1830. He learned that Offley supported the suspension of Nicholas Navoni as dragoman, a fact that would have given him greater hope for preferment as Navoni's successor. But at the ancient port, Hodgson had to face a reality that was a constant source of concern to diplomatists and commercial men in the Middle East. He arrived at Smyrna in the midst of a cholera epidemic; undoubtedly, this unhappy circumstance awoke memories of his arrival some months earlier in Constantinople. But he did not remain long in Smyrna, for he sailed on board the *Angelina*, a new ship with fine accommodations, on 16 October, bound for the port of Boston.[36] Hodgson arrived on 19 January 1832, and promptly conveyed news of his return to Secretary of State Livingston.[37]

Hodgson reached the United States at a time when the American people were deeply divided over the tariff question, one that would require Henry Clay, the Old Compromiser, to draft the tariff of 1833 to heal the wounds of division. But this did not greatly concern Hodgson, then intent on visiting his family at Richmond. His sojourn must have been one of anticipation, for he learned that General Jackson had put forward his name for the post of dragoman to succeed Nicholas Navoni, and he awaited Senate confirmation.[38] While at Richmond awaiting Senate action, Hodgson had two rather disagreeable matters of which to dispose. First, there was the difficulty caused by Navoni's charges against Commodore Porter. For having suspended him from the post of dragoman, Navoni sought revenge at Porter's expense. He charged him

with "disgraceful conduct" in the distribution of
presents at Constantinople. He also complained that
the Commodore had dismissed him without just cause.[39]
To counter Navoni's charges, Hodgson wrote Secretary
Livingston of the circumstances surrounding the
baseless charges. He admitted that Porter was un-
familiar with usage in the distribution of presents.
Apparently the Commodore had alotted insufficient
gifts for the Capudan Pacha, an oversight that was
immediately remedied by Porter. Thus, Hodgson could
advise the Secretary that this charge was in fact
without foundation. Hodgson turned to the question
of suspension, saying that Porter had taken this action due to Navoni's misconduct.[40]

The second matter of concern to Hodgson was Major
Henry Lee's unwillingness to pay Hodgson $1,153.00
for furniture and paintings that Hodgson had sold to
Lee on his arrival at Algiers. Hodgson informed the
Secretary that he had accepted Lee's note for the sum
and had requested Lee's authority to have his note
placed to his credit on the books of the Treasury Department.[41] Although a close friend of President
Jackson, Lee was probably not the best risk. His
star was on the wane, for he failed to obtain Senate
confirmation of his appointment as Consul General at
Algiers, and he had gone to live in Paris where he
engaged in literary pursuits to support himself.

Ultimately, Senate confirmation of his position in
late March, 1832, prompted Hodgson to prepare for the
long return voyage to Constantinople. He departed
for Boston in the latter days of March, arriving in
the New England port on 1 April. He sailed on the
brig *Tenedos* on 6 April, bound for the Turkish port of
Smyrna. He arrived in early June and traveled overland to the Turkish capital in a matter of eight
days.[42]

Hodgson's arrival at Constantinople found Commodore
Porter continuing to reside at Byuckdere. The Commodore's household now included John Porter Brown, one
of his nephews, who was now acting as the old man's

secretary. Brown had replaced George Porter, another of the Commodore's nephews who had come out to Constantinople with him in 1831, but was now serving as acting Consul to Morocco at Tangier.[43] That the Commodore was willing to employ his nephews in government service was a bad omen for Hodgson, whose career had depended upon his own talents and the assistance of high government officials who recognized his innate ability in the acquisition of Oriental languages. However, during Hodgson's early days with the Commodore all went well, and the Virginian soon found himself deeply immersed in the problem of the Turkish violation of the Treaty of 1830.

It seems that the Turks committed a breach of the treaty with the United States by charging American ships a duty of fifteen percent, while charging the most-favored nations only three percent.[44] The Commodore promptly ordered Hodgson to visit the Reis Effendi, lodge a complaint against this violation of the treaty, ascertan the motive for the additional charge, and finally to assert that the United States expected nothing less than most-favored-nation treatment.[45] The post papers of the American mission indicate that Hodgson diligently pursued his assigned task. His notes to the Commodore indicate nothing less than strict compliance with the latter's instructions.[46] Ultimately, Hodgson succeeded. Visiting the Reis Effendi in his villa on the Bosporus, Hodgson asked the Turkish official to permit the United States to use the French tariff and to abolish the fifteen percent tariff.[47] The Reis Effendi agreed, and on 16 August Hodgson translated from the Turkish to the English the Turk's reply granting the reduction in the tariff. Hodgson forwarded news of the event to the Commodore, signing his letter as "Secretary of Legation and Interpreter."[48] Commodore Porter notified Secretary Livingston that the tariff problem had been settled to his satisfaction, because Hodgson had carried out his instructions. He called attention to Hodgson's having translated the note from the Sublime Porte from Turkish into English.[49] Although Hodgson fulfilled his initial task in a manner that reflected the Commodore's unqualified satisfaction, things were soon to change the relationship between the former naval person and the aspiring Hodgson.

John Porter Brown was assisting the Commodore with correspondence, but his handwriting left much to be desired, and in November 1832 George Porter arrived from Tangier to assist the Commodore. The latter did not have much ability in acquiring languages, but he wrote a legible hand. Porter then decided to prepare Brown for a career as an interpreter. He chose Halim Effendi, the head of a large Muslim school in Constantinople. Halim was no doubt recommended to him by the Reverend Mr. William Goodell, an American missionary closely associated with Porter. During the ensuing years, except for a brief interlude, Brown pursued the study of language and gave considerable attention to the learning of Turkish customs and culture.[50] That the Commodore was guilty of rank nepotism is the opinion of his latest biographer, David F. Long, who wrote that Porter was "an open, unabashed, and usually successful nepotist on behalf of his sister's children."[51] But Hodgson stood in the way of the Commodore's plans. Porter, who at the close of his career would have four of his nephews on his staff at Constantinople, communicated to the Secretary of State his intention of placing George Brown on the payroll along with his other nephew, John Porter Brown. He avowed that the services of these two men "were very necessary to me," and that "I shall make them a small allowance . . . out of the contingent fund. It is my intention that both these young gentlemen shall devote their whole attention to the acquirement of a knowledge of the languages of the Orient, to the Turkish character, and manner of doing business, and of the customs and usage of diplomacy for which there is no better school than Constantinople."[52] Hodgson had a real problem on his hands, for he not only had to contend with the Commodore's two nephews, but he also had to deal with a bad-tempered old man who was notorious for his inability to get along with people.

Porter's nature has been described as that of a martinet, one who required that his every wish be met immediately. His household was run strictly along the lines prescribed for an American man-of-war. His petty, quarrelsome disposition was easily offended by the slightest infraction of what he considered to be proper etiquette. Porter's feuds were widespread. He did not get along with Captains James Biddle and Jesse D. Elliott, both of the U.S. Navy. The diplomatic corps at Constantinople did not like the Commodore.[53] Indeed, William N. Churchill, U.S. Consul at Constantinople, referred to Hodgson and others as his "fellow sufferers" from the Commodore's willful disposition.[54] Oddly enough, I have found only one positive description of Commodore David Porter. Elizabeth Kirkland of Boston recorded that he was a "warm hearted, social man," and "he makes a good deal of society of our missionaries, particularly Mr. and Mrs. Goodell."[55]

In November 1832 Commodore Porter removed to the suburb of Pera, a more fashionable quarter of Constantinople and one that was more suitable to a representative of the United States. But he was not without problems, for the plague had struck his household, carrying off one of his servants. To make matters worse, the Commodore himself came down with a bout with the plague. But it was to his household in Pera that George Porter returned to resume his duties on the Commodore's staff, a turn of events that had evil portents for Hodgson. Not only did Hodgson have to face the perils of the bubonic plague, but he also was compelled to compete with the Commodore's two nephews, whose claim to office was based solely on their blood relationship to the old man.[56] But the bad feeling that developed between Hodgson and Porter and his nephews was simply symptomatic of weaknesses in the American consular service during the 19th century. Porter, a political appointee with little or no claim to diplomatic expertise, had provided places for his nephews in a manner not unlike the local political boss passing out patronage to relatives or friends. By 1832 Hodgson had spent a considerable number of years in the service in the Middle East, was conversant with diplomatic customs and usage, had a fair command of Oriental languages, and could claim far more experience than the Commodore and his nephews combined. Nevertheless, the Commodore had the appointment of Chargé, enjoyed the good favor of General Jackson, and his word was law.

In December 1832 Hodgson, threatened with the two nephews, wrote the first of a long series of complaints to the Department of State, pointing out Porter's abuse of office. His initial complaint carried word that Commodore Porter was making room on his staff for John Porter Brown and for George Porter, with the latter being slated to hold down the post of Secretary of Legation, while the former was intended for a course of language study in Turkish. Hodgson noted that neither was possessed of a capacity for Turkish studies, because "they have no classical and but an imperfect English education. Without early discipline in the Latin and Greek languages," Hodgson wrote, "no man can attain a competent knowledge of Turkish. The only dictionary of this language is in Latin. Our universities furnish young men as highly educated as the *jeunes de langues* (young language students) sent here by European Governments, and unless such be sent by ours, we shall never have qualified Dragomans." He suggested that Arabic and Persian "must be studied contemporaneously with Turkish." In addition, the student should have a knowledge of French, Italian, and Greek. He complained that one nephew was assuming the office of Secretary of Legation, and the other, only nineteen years of age, was taking on duties that required a knowledge of commerce, law, and diplomatic usage. In addition to his complaint of nepotism, Hodgson argued that Porter should reorganize his mission to include a chancellor, skilled in law and commerce.[57]

While other factors would enter into the break between Hodgson and Porter, it is quite apparent that the latter's insistence on promoting the careers of his nephews at the former's expense was the major cause of the breach. So disgusted had Hodgson become over the Commodore's exclusion of him from the affairs of the Legation that his letter of complaint of 7 December carried the urgent request that he be transferred to Algiers or be given one of the Barbary consulates. Hodgson lamented the Commodore's giving the work to his two nephews, saying that they did not correspond with American commercial agents in French or Italian, as was customary, but in English; they then asked the agents to have the communiqués translated. He raised a question about Porter's expenditure of public funds to support members of his own family. Hodgson concluded his note with a word of self-approbation, saying that he felt qualified to assume the role of consul in any of the Barbary states where his language study would stand him in good stead. He mentioned that he maintained a regular correspondence with several Asiatic societies in Europe.[58]

If nepotism was the initial cause of Hodgson's differences with Porter, certainly his continued pleading with the Commodore to reorganize the American Legation was another bone of contention. Having served at Algiers as the Chargé and as Secretary under William Shaler, Hodgson had very definite ideas about the administration of affairs in the Legation. His experiences recently broadened by a visit to Greece to determine the conditions in that war-torn country,[59] Hodgson desired on his return to Constantinople to put the Legation's work on a more professional basis. He made numerous innovations with respect to the keeping of records, the issuance of requests for firmans or permits from the Turks that American ships might sail, and other changes that would streamline the Legation's routine procedures. Porter reprimanded Hodgson, asserting that the business of the Legation should be permitted to go on through the same channels as before and that no innovations may be made without his express approval.[60] Porter's rebuke reflected an authoritarian attitude gleaned from years of naval service. While the Commodore might have been remiss in his administration of the affairs of the Legation--a condition that resulted in the misnumbering of his dispatches-- he nevertheless strictly observed protocol and usage in another area. Archibald Turnbull recorded that "Daily at eight in the morning, as ceremoniously as though still commanding a ship of war, he made colors with his lodge-keeper and two Turkish guards. Woe betide the little party if the flag were not rounded chock-up and smartly belayed."[61] The feud between the Commodore and his dragoman extended into the next year, with the latter claiming that the services of Ascaroglou, the Armenian who served as second dragoman, were not needed due to the limited amount of business transacted between the American Legation and the Sublime Porte. When Hodgson so apprised Porter, the Commodore assumed his sternest quarterdeck manner and dressed Hodgson down in best naval tradition.[62] Although Porter did not then accept Hodgson's advice, he subsequently dismissed the Armenian and replaced him with one of his numerous relations.[63]

If Hodgson's suggestions to reorganize the American Legation initiated the feud between Hodgson and his superior, certainly the question of the visit of an American warship to Constantinople widened the cleavage between the two men and hardened the feeling of enmity. Porter ordered Hodgson to approach the Reis Effendi, requesting a firman for an American warship to come to Constantinople to protect American citizens and property.[64] The reason underlying this request was motivated by the complications growing out of the Greek War of Independence. Sultan Mahmud faced rebellion and a possible attack from Muhammad Ali, his vassal in Egypt. For aiding the Sultan during the Greek War of Independence, the Sultan granted Muhammad Ali the right to annex Crete and the promise of a governorship of the Peloponnesus for his son Ibrahim. But the Sultan was unable to keep his promise about the Peloponnesus, for the European Powers established the Kingdom of Greece. Muhammad Ali then turned his eyes to Syria, requesting that land as compensation for his son. On Sultan Mahmud's refusal, Muhammad Ali began his march on Syria, taking first Acre, then Damascus, Aleppo, Adana, and Konya and defeated the Turkish army decisively. Mahmud asked the European Powers for help, but only Russia replied by sending in early 1833 a fleet to the Bosporus with 14,000 Russian marines to secure Russian lives and property.[65]

Hodgson promptly repaired to the office of the Reis Effendi to obtain the firman. He was then informed that a reply would be forthcoming in a few days.[66] But the Commodore became impatient when the Reis Effendi refused to give a prompt reply to Hodgson's request. He became distraught and apparently used this delay as a rationale for venting his spleen on Hodgson.[67] The Turkish official gave a reply, saying that he could not permit an American warship to pass the Straits for the protection of American citizens, but he could allow it to pass on the need to acquire "friendly intelligence."[68] Porter lost control of himself, and used this instance to reprimand Hodgson for not setting forth properly the question of an American warship proceeding to the Turkish capital for the explicit reason that he had given at the outset. He wrote: "One would think, Sir, that the performance of the duty of asking a question . . . was a very simple affair. . . ."[69] Following a further exchange that included a second reprimand, Hodgson advised Porter that the Reis Effendi would issue a firman for an American frigate to pass the Dardanelles and that it would be issued immediately. But Hodgson remonstrated with his superior, asserting that the episode had placed him in an embarrassing situation, for the diplomatic usages of the Sublime Porte "must be consulted and respected where they affect neither the honor nor the interests of our country."[70] Porter was beside himself with rage on receiving Hodgson's response. As if ordering a seaman to mount the yardarm in the midst of a storm, the old man commanded Hodgson to go directly to the Porte to obtain the firman for the American warship and then transmit it immediately to him.[71] Hodgson threw caution to the winds, replying that the dignity of the dragomannic office demanded the use of a campou aghlan or servant of the Legation, to obtain firmans from the Porte. Tossing the fat in the fire, Hodgson admonished the Commodore, saying he was sure that he would not want to demean him by such a task.[72] The feud had reached a fever pitch, but the Commodore delayed giving a reply to Hodgson. In about two weeks he asserted that he disliked the hostile attitude that Hodgson had allegedly assumed toward him. He rebuked Hodgson sharply, writing, "the services rendered by you to this Legation are not so important as to make it necessary that I should add in any way to its expenses for your accommodation or your dignity as requested by your note. . . ."[73] Hodgson did not get his dignity soothed with the services of a messenger, and, inasmuch as Commodore Porter now lived at San Stefano, some ten miles from the city, Hodgson complained to Secretary of State Livingston that he was compelled to make the long trip by boat from the Commodore's residence to the Sublime Porte in order to obtain firmans for American ships. This, Hodgson pointed out, caused a considerable delay to American merchant ships.[74]

By the spring of 1833 the enmity between Hodgson and his superior had reached a high plateau, causing Hodgson to submit a second request for a transfer from the American Legation at Constantinople to some post in the Barbary states.[75] While it would appear that Porter was on the surface dismayed with Hodgson's improper performance of his duties, the presence of the Commodore's nephews in the Legation would suggest that his petty fault-finding with Hodgson's routine work was a mere chimera covering his deep devotion to his family and his determination to further their interests at the expense of Hodgson's career. Nepotism was a great evil that plagued the American government both in its domestic agencies in Washington and in its foreign service. The lack of a professional body of foreign service officers permitted a man to abuse the system by placing his relatives on the payroll. Hodgson was more the victim of a faulty system than of the displeasure of an irascible old man whose predilection for power and family preferment worked to his disadvantage.

Even so, Hodgson, having earned the disapprobation of Commodore Porter in the matter of the firman for the American warship, soon found himself embroiled with his bad-tempered superior in another episode involving the price of fees for firmans for American merchant ships. It seems that an M. S. Cohen, an American from Baltimore, complained to the Commodore that the price of firmans between November, 1831, and the spring of 1833 had more than doubled in price from 33 piastres to 80 piastres. Given the fact that the British charged only 12 piastres, Cohen had serious reason to question the abrupt increase in price.[76] Porter replied that the price charged was in line with those charged by other legations in Constantinople. He said that Hodgson had determined the price, based on information secured by him, and that if any overcharge was involved that Hodgson was to blame. He wrote subsequently that the fee included the charges of the Porte, a fee for boat hire, a charge for the campou aghlan or messenger, and a small charge for the second dragoman. These fees, Porter asserted, accounted for 50 piastres.[77] Cohen's response was curt and to the point. He bitterly complained that Porter's explanation did not satisfy him. He said the Commodore's charge did not account for the difference between 50 and 80 piastres.[78] It was at this juncture that Hodgson saw fit to complain to the Secretary of State. He explained that Cohen had lodged a grievance at the Legation about the increased price of firmans, which had doubled between 1831 and 1833. Hodgson suggested that the high price was charged to defray the costs of the Commodore's two nephews who were now on the Legation's payroll. He postulated that the nephews were definitely paid out of the Legation's contingency fund, but that the second dragoman was left virtually unpaid. He was compelled to live on the fee that he received for obtaining firmans from the Porte.[79]

Undoubtedly Hodgson's complaint to Secretary Livingston was more than the Commodore could stand, for it was at about this time that Porter removed Hodgson as Secretary of Legation. The old man wrote that his patience was at an end, that he could no longer look kindly on him, and that his duties were now limited to act as interpreter between himself and the Sublime Porte.[80] Hodgson acted quickly, writing to the Secretary that Porter had indeed removed him from the office of Secretary of Legation. He averred that he had always respected Porter, but since the Commodore had insulted him in March, he had "abstained from going to his house." He said that the charges lodged against him were groundless and that he feared they were trumped up in order that he will "ultimately be sacrificed to the Commodore's nephews." Hodgson pleaded with the Secretary to restore him to the clerkship which he held in the Department prior to his departure for Constantinople.[81] Subsequently, Hodgson reminded the Secretary of State that the title "Secretary of Legation," with all of its functions, was conferred on him by the Secretary of State. Hodgson asserted that the title belonged to him until such time as the Secretary should see fit to revoke it. Hodgson lamented that the Commodore would not permit him to exchange places with George Brown, U.S. Consul at Algiers, for "he wanted something for those boys--his nephews." He declared that Porter had limited his duties to those of dragoman, but that he permitted the second dragoman to handle most of the business with the Porte. Hodgson complained finally that the Legation was poorly organized and that the Commodore charged double the ordinary price for the issuance of firmans.[82] The following month Hodgson wrote the Department, complaining that the Commodore would no longer permit him to see dispatches sent to Washington and that this was a violation of the instructions that the Department had drawn up to guide the efforts of secretaries of legation.[83] It seems that Secretary of State Martin Van Buren had issued a circular in 1830, describing the duties of secretaries of legation. These included the transcription, copying, and recording of dispatches and other communications sent out from the legation.[84] Porter was not long in answering Hodgson's charges. He wrote him on 20 June, asserting

that the title of "Secretary of Legation" as expressly
defined in a letter from Secretary of State Livingston
on 3 April 1832, did not apply to Hodgson. By law,
Porter remonstrated, the title is only given to those
missions that are lead by a minister plenipotentiary.
Porter asserted that the title "Secretary of Legation"
had not been given to Hodgson and that his sole duty
was to serve as dragoman, a duty which did not call
for him to read the dispatches to the Secretary. Porter later informed Livingston that the title had been
given Hodgson merely to satisfy his own desires.[85] To
Secretary Livingston Porter addressed the complaint
that Hodgson had not only insisted on exercising the
duties of secretary, but that he had tried "to assume
to himself the exercise of my duties." He accused
Hodgson of assuming an importance to his person which
had caused others in the diplomatic corps to ridicule
him.[86]

In charging Hodgson with pretensions and arrogance,
Porter thereby inserted another factor into the continuing feud. Writing Livingston, Porter noted that
Hodgson had "silly ambitions of being thought the
only person in this Legation capable of conducting its
affairs with dignity." For example, he stated that he
had sent Hodgson to call on the French Minister when
he (Porter) was too ill to make the social call. He
observed that Hodgson made the call "in his own person
or on his own account." He reiterated that the Secretary of the French Legation then returned a card to
Hodgson and that a coolness had developed between himself and the French Minister, until he explained the
situation. Further, he observed that Hodgson had
made numerous visits to "Turkish dignitaries" on his
own account" and not as the duly authorized representative of the Chargé. Finally, he related that
Hodgson had called on the French poet, Baron Lamartine,
claiming that he was the former "American Consul General at Algiers."[87] It would appear that perhaps Hodgson acted in a manner unbefitting one who had so long
served in the service of his country. But given the
reality that Porter had lodged the complaint, there is
the possibility that the Commodore was overstating the
case in order to put Hodgson in a bad light, thereby

Constantinople 71

paving the way for his nephews at Hodgson's expense.
There is little doubt that Hodgson's behavior indicates a personality that was keenly aware of position and dignity and that he was given to playing the role of consular officer with all of the privileges associated with the title. But inasmuch as he had had years of experience at Algiers, one can question the Commodore's accusations. Nevertheless, Hodgson did feel intensely the loss of position, for, as he complained to the Commodore, he had attended a fête of the Russian Envoy and learned from the members of the diplomatic corps that he was not expected to be there. He related that an Austrian diplomatic official told him that he was excluded from diplomatic society because he was no longer considered a secretary of legation. Hodgson lamented that he was now excluded from the society of the diplomatic corps.[88] Porter replied that he had been invited to the Russian fête along with all members of the Legation because he (Porter) had used his good offices to have him included. But he revealed that he had not been invited to social functions at the Austrian and Prussian legations because he no longer served the American Legation as its secretary. Porter also asserted that his exclusion might well have been due to Hodgson's unseemly conduct on the Champ de Mort as typical of the bad name which he said Hodgson had with the diplomatic corps. Porter claimed that he found it difficult to believe the current report that he (Hodgson) had struck a gentleman with his riding whip while riding and that he had then fled to escape punishment.[89] Hodgson replied that he had met a friend of his while out riding and that his friend, while under the influence of champagne, had jumped up on his horse and "done many foolish things." Hodgson elaborated: "I cracked his knuckles to make him dismount, but he "struck me in the face. I returned the blow," Hodgson related, "and then left the scene." He revealed that his friend was Consul Cartwright at the British Embassy, who would gladly verify that he (Hodgson) had never created such a scene in the first place.[90]

If the loss of his title of Secretary of Legation caused Hodgson much pain, the loss of his post of dragoman cost him even greater anguish, for he realized that the Commodore's nephews had now entirely replaced him. As early as March of 1833 Commodore Porter had written Secretary of State Livingston that he would soon have to dispense with Hodgson's services as interpreter.[91] By June of that year, Porter had cause to question Hodgson's proficiency in Turkish. Writing the Secretary of State, Porter exclaimed that his interpreter had to rely on a dictionary to translate from Turkish into English and that in his opinion he would require years of study to achieve the knowledge of the second dragoman. In making this assessment, Porter acknowledged that he knew no Arabic or Turkish.[92] By the following month, Porter had begun to rely on Ascaroglou, the second dragoman, and he so informed the Secretary in a devastating indictment of Hodgson's ability as an interpreter. In what amounts to an impeachment of the young Virginian's use of Turkish, Porter wrote that in his opinion not only was Hodgson incompetent to act as dragoman, but that this estimate was shared by Turkish officials at the Porte. He simply does "not understand the Turkish language," Porter declared, and "it gives me pain to be under the necessity of exposing an imposter, but duty requires that I make knowledge to the Department that Mr. Hodgson is one who pretends to a sufficient knowledge of the Turkish language to enable him to perform, unassisted, the duties of Dragoman." In closing, Porter divulged that he had removed Hodgson as dragoman, alleging that Hodgson "has brought ridicule and contempt on himself by his behavior," and he hoped that he will not find "new ways of vexing and embarrassing me."[93] Having informed the Department of his action, Porter wrote Hodgson, announcing that "you are totally incompetent when unassisted to perform the duties of First Dragoman to the Legation." For that reason he had removed Hodgson as Dragoman and had so apprised the Reis Effendi and the Department. He wrote that he had as yet not asked the American bankers in London to decline honoring drafts drawn by him to defray expenses and salary.[94]

Hodgson wrote to Louis McLane, who had succeeded Edward Livingston as Secretary of State on 29 May 1833, complaining that the Commodore had removed him from the office of Secretary to the Legation and from that of First Dragoman. He bewailed the reality that he would soon share the fate of Nicholas Navoni, his predecessor. Fearing that the Commodore would soon remove him from the Legation's pay roll, Hodgson disclosed that the older man had also accused him of a "breach of confidence and of incompetency in his office." In conclusion, Hodgson affirmed his readiness and willingness to perform the duties of his office, and that for the present he would remain at his quarters in Pera to await information and future disposition of his case.[95] Hodgson's fears proved valid, for on 3 August Porter wrote Hodgson that he had communicated with Baring Brothers, the American bankers in London, and disclosed to them that he had removed him from the office of dragoman as of 11 July and left it up to them to honor the future drafts submitted by him.[96] Somewhat later, Hodgson wrote McLane, apprising him that W. N. Churchill, the American Consul at Constantinople, now acted as mediary between himself and the Commodore, with whom he no longer communicated. Porter had removed him from his office, acted to sever his pay and allowances, and would no longer receive him; hence the necessity of using an intermediary.[97]

What can be said of the feud between Porter and Hodgson? Was it based purely on personality differences? Did the Commodore's penchant for nepotism color his opinion of Hodgson in order to drive him from the Legation to secure place and preferment for one of his relatives? Was there good reason for the Commodore to doubt Hodgson's proficiency in the use of Turkish? An examination of the case reveals some interesting insights into a situation in the American Legation at Constantinople that point out several glaring weaknesses in the selection process or lack of process used by the Department of State to obtain staff for its consular service.

    This much can be said on Hodgson's behalf. He had remained at Algiers for three years, during which time he avidly pursued the study of Arabic and Turkish, in addition to Berber. Officials at the Department of State had confidence in his ability to use Turkish. In the instructions given Commodore Porter to effect the exchange of ratifications, Martin Van Buren wrote: "from his intelligence, discretion, and experience, and his acquaintance with the Turkish character and habits, added to his knowledge of the Arabic and Turkish languages, acquired by his residence at Algiers, there is every reason to believe that you would find him very useful, and that you will be glad of the opportunity of having the benefit of his company and assistance."[98] It will also be recalled that Porter had written the Department, extolling Hodgson's abilities and recommending him for the post of dragoman at Constantinople. Concerning his use of Turkish, Hodgson himself wrote to Edward Livingston, saying, "For ordinary purposes, I can write Turkish, and may write it well. If Com. Porter has any doubts of this, I should be most happy to be examined by the savants at Paris."[99] Too, if Hodgson were so dependent upon Ascaroglou, the second dragoman, as Porter avowed, why was Hodgson so desirous of having him removed from the staff of the Legation? Without the assistance of the Armenian, he would then no longer be able to function effectively. In addition, it should be noted that Porter had good cause to have Hodgson removed. His biographer, David F. Long, has certainly presented a strong case condemning Porter as a nepotist. Long pointed out that at his death the Commodore had four nephews on his Legation staff, necessitating his juggling Legation funds to support these men. One of them, Samuel D. Heap, Jr., served as a dragoman, yet knew no foreign language whatsoever. Porter's dim view of Hodgson and his determination to be rid of him is colored by a letter to Commodore Daniel Patterson in 1835, in which he referred to Hodgson as "incorrigible." A second letter to Senator Mahlon Dickerson described Hodgson as a "spy,"[100] leading us to believe that Hodgson was in the pay of some foreign government.

But there is sufficient evidence on the negative side to suggest that Hodgson had inadequate training to translate the Turco-American Treaty from the Turkish into the English. In the monumental collection, Treaties and Other International Acts of the United States of America, edited by David Hunter Miller, there is good evidence to suggest that Hodgson was not as accomplished in his use of the Turkish language as he himself claimed. During his stay at the Department of State, he made five translations of the treaty, each represented as being made from the Turkish. Examination of the translations suggests that Hodgson used a French translation and Navoni's translation from the Turkish to render his translations into English. His last translation indicates that he could read Turkish to "some extent," but not completely, and that he "could, in part and with errors, translate what he read."[101] Regarding this translation, Hodgson wrote that he made it in 1832 and that he had made extensive use of Arabic-Turkish-Persian Lexicon prepared by Mesgnient Meninski, first published in 1680-1687.[102] Moreover, Hodgson's translation of the Turkish instrument of ratification is found to be "a very imperfect rendering of the Turkish, both in respect of errors and of omissions."[103]

There is little need to doubt the Department of State's conclusion that Hodgson's use of Turkish in the early 1830s left something to be desired. But a question needs to be raised? Could it be that Hodgson overstated his ability to use Turkish in order to ensure his place and advancement in the consular service at a time when the Department had no rationalized system for the procurement of a qualified body of men for the service? The absence of a system required the aspiring professional to support his cause with the endorsements of persons highly placed in whatever administration then holding the White House. Perhaps the lack of an orderly method of advancement, the payment of insufficient salaries, the absence of a career service, and the overall amateurish nature of the nation's representatives overseas compelled many to overcharge fees for the rendering of consular services and to make claims to expertise in language in order to survive in chaotic circumstances. Hodgson's guilt was perhaps no less than that of Commodore Porter, who practiced nepotism, or than those consuls who overcharged for consular services or abused the system of capitulations by selling protection to Ottoman citizens then employed as dragomans, consular agents, clerks, guards, and the like. The lack of a system for its consular officers led the officials in the Department of State to consider reforms of the defects in the consular system. In 1833 Edward Livingston made an abortive effort to reform the deficiencies in the system,[104] a fact in extenuation of Hodgson's inflated claims. Nevertheless, this need of reform does not excuse his actions.

The widening breach between Hodgson and Porter must have proven an embarrassment to officials at the Department of State who were receiving Porter's dispatches describing the need to remove Hodgson. At the time, they received communiqués from Hodgson, advising of alleged wrong doings on the part of Commodore Porter. Writing on 8 May 1833, Hodgson set forth the facts of an episode responsible for deepening the cleavage between the Commodore and his former dragoman--one that brought discredit to the Chargé d'Affaires. It appears that Henry Eckford contracted with the Turks to provide live oak timber for the construction of a ship of war. The Turks advanced the sum of $40,000.00 for the cost of the timber, while Henry Eckford agreed to pay the freight. Eckford died, and Porter was given power of attorney to act as administrator of the estate. Three ships (one British and two American) arrived at Constantinople with the timber. Porter demanded that the Turks pay the freight before delivery, whereupon the captains refused, claiming that the Turkish Government was not responsible for defraying the freight charges. They claimed Porter was answerable for paying the $10,000.00 charge. Porter replied that he had no funds of Eckford's to pay. But Hodgson affirmed that the Commodore, while acting for

Eckford's heirs, had just shipped a consignment of opium worth $50,000.00 to the United States and that he should have paid the charges out of that profit. The British Chancery ruled on the matter, submitting that the case must pass to the Turkish courts. Hodgson advised the Secretary of State that Porter had made himself an agent for Eckford's heirs and had thereby compromised his ability to represent the American sea captains. He claimed that Porter had made a secret agreement with the Turks, which had not been submitted to the Senate, to supply them with timber and military supplies.[105] Subsequently, Hodgson divulged that the ships would not discharge their cargoes, that the Turks refused the captains the necessary firmans to sail, and that Porter would not terminate the matter by payment. He stated that the Commodore's acting for Eckford's heirs had "excited unfriendly feelings in this government, which I fear may be exhibited in the injury of our interests." He warned that Porter's failure to pay would result in a case before a Turkish tribunal which was contrary to the stipulations of the Turco-American Treaty. Hodgson claimed that by abandoning the American captains to a Turkish court Porter had violated the principle of extraterritoriality contained in the capitulatory rights. Hodgson concluded that Porter had arrogated responsibilities to himself that exceeded his authority as a representative of the United States Government, for by acting as the executor of Eckford's estate he had violated the principle of extraterritoriality. He noted that there was no law of Congress that could require an American citizen here to pay his debts, and that a minister cannot enforce justice among his fellow citizens.[106] Somewhat later Hodgson described a ludicrous situation in which Porter had placed himself.

It seems that Porter had been using Ascaroglou, the second dragoman, for some months "in dunning the officers of this Government for money, on account of Mr. Eckford's estate." Further, that "Eckford was in the service of a foreign power . . . and I do not believe such Agencies to be in the province of a Chargé d'Affaires, particularly in Turkey where he is an Officer of Justice."[107]

The Commodore found himself in difficulty with the Secretary of State, necessitating his giving a very long explanation of his involvement in the affairs of the late Henry Eckford. Writing to Louis McLane on 9 August 1833, Porter admitted that he was indeed acting for the heirs of Eckford. He wrote that no agreement had been found between Eckford and the Sultan regarding the sale of the timber. Inasmuch as Churchill, Bunker and Co. was the contractor of Mr. Eckford in the United States for delivery of the timber, Porter declared that he had arranged that the partners of this firm handle the landing of the timber. Porter set forth that he had reported to the Capudan Pacha that the timber had arrived, that Churchill, Bunker and Co. would discharge all of the cargoes, and that payment would be made for tools delivered by Eckford to the Turkish navy yard. The Capudan Pacha agreed that when the timber was landed, inspected and found to be in good condition, that the Sultan's government would settle all claims by Eckford's heirs against the government. Porter declared that he had announced this agreement to all parties concerned, but that the ship captains refused to unload their cargoes. Eventually, they agreed to unload the timber. It was inspected and found to be fit for use, and the Sultan's government paid the freight and claims of Eckford's estate.[108] The Secretary replied to Porter's explanation, asserting that there was some question in the Department about his connection with the Eckford estate, a factor that was causing the government some embarrassment. The President, McLane wrote, "desires that you dissolve the connection and confine yourself strictly to your official duties." He maintained that the Department did want to protect and expand American commerce and that Porter should communicate to the Department such information as may assist American business interests.[109] Although Porter was able

Constantinople 79

to make a valid explanation of his handling of the Eckford episode, nevertheless, it must have stirred up his ire to know that Hodgson was responsible for his mild dressing down at the hands of the Secretary of State.

But there was a final scene in the feud between the Commodore and his former dragoman. Porter wrote Hodgson on 28 October 1833, asserting that it was his understanding that Dr. Marino Lazzaro, physician to H. E. Salih Pasha, late Pasha of the Dardanelles, had given a horse to Hodgson which was to be presented to himself. The Commodore queried Hodgson on the whereabouts of the animal, saying he wished to inform the government in Washington and ask its instructions respecting the disposal of it.[110] Hodgson replied, using Commodore D. L. Patterson, the senior American Naval officer present at Constantinople, as an intermediary. He asked the Commodore to "shield him from unparalleled slander and oppression on the part of the Charge d'Affaires." Hodgson explained in the missive that he did indeed receive a horse from Dr. Lazzaro about six months ago and that the horse was valued at from thirty to forty dollars. He asserted that he had given the doctor a "full equivalent" in return for the animal and that he had a clear title to it.[111] Matters drew to a head when Porter requested Commodore Patterson to make Hodgson a prisoner to prevent him from doing "future mischief." The Commodore replied that he could not arrest Hodgson, for he was not "subject to martial law, nor was he accused of any criminal offense."[112] Hodgson at this juncture gave a sworn statement to Consul William Churchill, affirming that in late April or May he had received a horse, for which he gave a case of glassware to Dr. Lazzaro in payment for the horse. He admitted that he had sold the horse because it had weak forelegs--this on the advice of Mr. Vitalle, in whose Pera home he resided. Porter also made a sworn statement, claiming that the horse was his property, that Hodgson was a swindler, and that he was not a "fit companion for gentlemen because he imposes himself on society with titles which did not belong to him." These statements were rejected by Commodore Patterson who, wrote Porter that the wardroom officers of this frigate (the <u>United States</u>) "cannot retain charges of the most serious nature, unsubstantiated by any proof, reflecting upon a man /Hodgson/ with whom they have associated on terms of intimacy as a gentleman and as a man of honor."[113]

The contretemps between Porter and Hodgson became violent, for Hodgson had dined with the officers of the wardroom of the <u>U.S.S. Delaware</u>, and after the meal he and another person were rowed ashore in the barge of which Mr. David Porter was the officer-in-charge. On landing, Porter, the Commodore's son, assaulted Hodgson "for the trouble you have given my father." Porter struck him a violent blow on the head and hit him repeatedly. Hodgson fell to the ground, was subjected to numerous kicks by Porter, who evidently destroyed Hodgson's coat, and received a verbal tongue-lashing. Hodgson complained to Commodore Patterson, asking for retribution and punishment. While Midshipman Porter was not punished, he was required to pay Hodgson $35.00 for damage to his coat.[114]

Hodgson did not let the matter lie, for he informed the Secretary of State that Porter had called for his imprisonment for "horse-theft, swindling, forgery, and conduct unbecoming a gentleman." He observed that Midshipman Porter had assaulted him with no provocation. Inasmuch as Porter was both accuser and judge, Hodgson made his plea for a settlement of the affair, and he submitted to the Secretary sworn statements signed by Commodore Patterson, Captain J. L. Nicholson, and Lieutenant Veul, exonerating him of the charge of horse-theft.[115]

Unbeknown to Hodgson or Porter, the Secretary of State had already determined to remove Hodgson from the Legation at Constantinople and had dispatched orders directing him to proceed to Egypt on a secret mission. But before discussing Hodgson's interesting mission to the Land of the Nile, it is first necessary to conclude the difficulties between Hodgson and Porter. It seems that Porter had written Secretary of State John Forsyth, McLane's successor, urging that Hodgson be formally censured. Forsyth refused, observing: "If cause for censure had been perceived in your department towards Mr. Hodgson, you would have been informed of it by the Department, but as he was withdrawn from the Legation and all occasion of future difficulty was thereby removed, it was thought most conducive to the public interest that the matter should be dismissed without further discussion."[116] Although Hodgson did not receive a censure, Porter was rebuked by both McLane and Forsyth for his failure to number properly dispatches sent to the Department of State.[117] This is an ironic twist, for Hodgson had first called the Department's attention to the Commodore's malfeasance in administering the affairs of the Legation with regard to keeping proper records, numbering dispatches, and the like.

The whole sordid confrontation between Porter and Hodgson raises several important questions about the nature of the administration of the U.S. consular service in the nineteenth century. First, would the adversary relationship between the two men have arisen had the Department of State evolved a more rational system for the selection of its representatives and agents in overseas posts? Had this been the case, there would have been no possibility of Commodore Porter placing his nephews in the Legation at Hodgson's expense. Second, if the Department had established guidelines for the retention of its personnel on a permanent basis and for the professionalization of its agents, would Hodgson have been compelled to overstate his ability to use Turkish in order to further his career? Third, if Porter had not been able to place a nephew, John Porter Brown, in the Legation where he remained for many years as dragoman, would he have been able to earn the "distinction of having become the first Oriental language specialist in the Diplomatic Service,"[118] or would that distinction have been reserved for William Brown Hodgson?  At all events, the contretempts with Porter did not damage his career, and Hodgson rapidly made his plans to depart on his mission to Egypt, thankful to be rid of the domineering old man who had tried to damage his career.

# 5
# SECRET MISSION TO EGYPT

Chapter 5


The Secret Mission to Egypt


The confidence in the country's future overseas commercial expansion as expressed in the Turco-American Treaty of 1830 was also manifest in the Department of State's desire to increase commercial intercourse with Egypt. As will be recalled, the Middle East during the 1830s was in turmoil, for Muhammad Ali, the Ottoman Sultan's vassal in Egypt, had risen in rebellion. Having failed to receive fitting reward for his aid to the Sultan during the Greek War for Independence, Muhammad Ali turned his attention to Syria, which he claimed for his son Ibrahim. In 1833 peace between the Sultan and his rebellious viceroy was concluded, with Muhammad Ali holding Crete, Egypt, Syria, Adana, and Tarsus, in agreement for which he paid the Sultan some ₤150,000 per year in tribute. Thus to all intents and purposes it appeared that the vassal was an independent overlord in his own right. During the conflict between the Sultan and his vassal, Commodore Porter had ordered Commodore Patterson to deploy his squadron to the eastern Mediterranean to maintain surveillance over the on-going war.[1] Ever mindful of the American navy's role in trade expansion, Patterson viewed the situation with optimism. He wrote Secretary of

State Livingston that Muhammad Ali, Viceroy of Egypt, is independent and will "gladly enter into a commercial treaty with us." He advised that he hoped the Department of State would send instructions to him for the purpose of making a treaty with the Egyptian leader.[2]

This communication reached Livingston, who immediately leaped at the opportunity of solving his problem at Constantinople where Hodgson and Porter had reached an impasse, and, simultaneously pursuing the Jackson administration's penchant for overseas commercial expansion. His successor, Louis McLane, wrote Hodgson, saying that the President was disturbed by the lack of harmony between himself and Commodore Porter and that "without finally deciding upon your case, the President deems it proper to withdraw you from the Legation at Constantinople." He asserted that the President considered him to be "useful" and wished to employ him "in a different service of great trust and importance. . . ." "The Department," McLane wrote, "has decided to send you as a confidential agent" to Egypt to determine "how far it may be desirable and practicable to form commercial relations with the Pacha of that country, distinct from those with the Porte." He stated that Hodgson was to proceed "without delay to Egypt, there to determine Muhammad Ali's power to make commercial treaties, his disposition toward the United States, the extent of his having made treaties with European Powers, the status of the various consulates in Egypt, the condition of Egyptian trade and industry, the extent of its shipping, the kinds of its products, the nature and extent of the commerce it carried on with foreign countries, and finally "the best means to be adopted for extending and improving the commercial intercourse between the United States and the countries subject to the authority of the Pacha." Having gathered his information, Hodgson was ordered to make his recommendations and promptly return to Washington, where he was to present to the Department a detailed report on the subject. He allowed

Hodgson three months to complete his mission, which
was viewed as "strictly confidential," and ordered
him to obtain a copy of Porter's cypher in order to
communicate with the Department in secret. The sum
of $700.00 was considered ample for the mission, and
McLane ordered Hodgson to draw on Commodore Porter's
contingency fund.[3]

The Secretary's dispatch, accompanied by an explanatory dispatch to Commodore Porter,[4] found Hodgson exuberant over his turn of luck. He acknowledged his gratitude for the Department's "undiminished confidence" in him, saying that he was apprehensive, lest the difference with the Commodore should have resulted in his removal from the service. Anticipating future employment, Hodgson wrote that he had not been idle, but had spent his time studying Oriental languages.[5] Within the week, the grateful Hodgson submitted to the Secretary a preliminary report on the state of affairs in the Middle East, suggesting that he had made himself aware of the changing power configuration in that distant region. Reaffirming his appreciation for the new mission, he advised that Muhammad Ali hoped to add to the territory then under his control by bringing under his hegemony the Arabic-speaking peoples of the Middle East, as distinguished from the Turkish. He observed that the relative land and naval forces would show that the Sultan had an advantage, with some 69 ships in the Ottoman Navy as compared to 31 in that of Muhammad Ali. The Sultan had some 70,000 regular troops to match a like number for Muhammad Ali.[6]

Aware that his withdrawal from Constantinople was final and that his secret mission to Egypt was only of a temporary nature, Hodgson wrote to Judge McLean, with a view to keeping his political fences mended in order to ensure future employment by the Department of State. He informed his patron that he had been ordered to leave the Legation at Constantinople on a "special mission," the purpose of which he could not then reveal. He brought McLean up to date on his situation at the Ottoman capital, lamenting the fact that Porter had mistreated him in the manner for which he was well known. He said that Porter had made "violent scenes" in Constantinople and that his conduct was shameful. Because the Jackson administration had been fair to him, he suggested that he could not too readily expose Porter's misconduct and he hoped McLean would not divulge the contents of his letter. Indicating that he had not spent his time in idleness, Hodgson concluded with the statement that he could not help but relate that he could now translate letters from the Sultan of Turkey, the Pacha of Egypt, the Shah of Iran, and the King of Greece.[7] This latter statement was included to impress McLean, with the hope that he could continue to stand by him in the pursuit of his career at the Department of State.

Eager to make a record that would remove any doubts about his competence in the Deparment, Hodgson kept the Secretary informed of conditions in the Middle East. He submitted a second summary of events in the Levant, indicating a keen grasp of the complicated facets of the Near Eastern Question that had plagued European chancelleries for many years and would aggravate European statesmen for decades to come. With respect to relations between Muhammad Ali and the Sublime Porte, he observed that "opinion is entertained here that a rupture . . . is as inevitable as is his independence sure." He noted that he was then prepared to embark on his mission, having just returned from an excursion through the Balkans, Romelia, Adrianople, and a brief sea voyage through the Black Sea. He gave as the reason for his absence from Constantinople the continued suffering from gastroenteritis. Hodgson assured the Secretary that he would preserve the "confidential character of my mission" by travelling as a "private gentleman" through Syria and Egypt. He said he would obtain the customary firmans given to travellers and that he could detect no suspicion of his mission by his colleagues. He would travel to Smyrna and there charter a small vessel to take him to Alexandria. Inasmuch as he desired to know the extent of Muhammad Ali's power, he advised that he would touch certain Syrian ports. He admitted that his anticipated expenses would approximate $700.00, but he bemoaned the niggardliness of Commodore Porter who would allow him only $500.00.[8]

To the very end, Porter intensely disliked Hodgson, a feeling exhibited in a letter to his wife, Evelina, in which he wrote "my mind is more at ease, I have not that puppy Hodgson to vex me."[9] Although the ill-tempered Porter gave Hodgson but $500.00 for his mission, nevertheless, Secretary of State John Forsyth later informed the Commodore that Hodgson's mission to Egypt resulted in expenses of $774.16 which had been defrayed out of Porter's contingency fund. Forsyth advised the Commodore that he should deduct the amount from his account in London.[10]

Hodgson's trip across Anatolia to Smyrna must have been uneventful, for he recorded no untoward incidents in his reports to the State Department. He arrived at Alexandria on 24 August, having touched at the islands of Stanchio, Rhodes, and Cyprus, and made a brief visit to Beirut, the Syrian port of entry. At Alexandria the Egyptian authorities required him to endure a rigorous 21-day quarantine. It was late in September before he was able to take those steps necessary to fulfill his instructions.

In the process of carrying out his task, Hodgson submitted to the Department two initial reports, one preliminary report, and a final detailed accounting of his mission. Writing to Secretary of State McLane on 25 August 1834, while still in quarantine, Hodgson disclosed that Muhammad Ali had sailed with his fleet from Alexandria to support his son Ibrahim in Palestine, but that he had returned to Egypt following the pacification of Jaffa. He now awaited the arrival of the Sultan's fleet, which was reputed moving to attack his forces in order to restore Syria to the Ottoman Empire. He divulged that the Egyptian leader "presents the phenomenon not uncommon in the Ottoman annals of a prince de facto independent and de nomine subject to the Sublime Porte, paying no assessed tribute, and yet making large voluntary presents." This status, Hodgson claimed, amounted to "quasi independence." With respect to Egyptian commerce, he observed that early reports indicated a bountiful harvest due to an unusually heavy inundation of the Nile River. The cotton crop was estimated to run to 25 million pounds, while the opium crop, new for Egypt, was expected to be extensive. He announced that a small commerce already existed between Alexandria and the United States, with the enterprising house of Stith and Company of Smyrna carrying on trade in lignum vitae and mahogany.[11]

Having endured his quarantine, Hodgson got down to work. He immediately contacted John Gliddon, the English merchant who served as the American consular agent at Alexandria, to arrange for interviews with Muhammad Ali and Boghos Bey, the Egyptian Minister of Foreign Affairs and Director of Exterior Commerce. Gliddon was sympathetic and cooperative, for the records of the American Legation at Constantinople reveal several interesting reports on commerce emanating from Gliddon and carrying the suggestion that the United States might find it advantageous to pursue expanded commercial intercourse with Egypt. In his second report to the Department, Hodgson addressed himself to commercial, political, and diplomatic affairs. He related that he had had two interviews with Muhammad Ali, with Boghos Bey in attendance. The result was highly satisfactory, for the Egyptian head of state expressed the view that closer ties might obtain between the United States and Egypt and that a commercial treaty might be forthcoming. With respect to the international political situation, Hodgson reported that the British and French had persuaded Sultan Mahmoud to suspend military operations for the present, but that war was undoubtedly in the offing. With regard to the American consular agent,

Hodgson disclosed that John Gliddon was an English merchant who had difficulty with the British Consul General, who asserted his jurisdiction over Gliddon. Boghos Bey had suggested that Gliddon should no longer continue as consular agent. However, Commodore Porter approved Gliddon's continuation at his post at Alexandria.[12] This latter conclusion would suggest that Hodgson wanted to create a position for himself, and, indeed, that is exactly the conclusion reached by David Finnie.[13]

But Hodgson did not confine his stay in Egypt to Alexandria, for he visited Cairo, the Egyptian capital, where George R. Gliddon, son of John Gliddon, arranged for him to meet Habib Effendi, the Lieutenant Governor. The latter gave him a thorough survey of Egyptian resources. Hodgson exultantly exclaimed that "Our conversation was held in Turkish, and his expressions of pleasure from that circumstance, were flattering to me. It is singular, he said, that you, from the New World, should have taken the rare pains to study my language."[14] From Cairo, Hodgson traveled up the Nile as far as the sugar refinery of Radamon. He also visited several cotton factories along the way.

Having inspected the important agricultural regions of the country, talked to high government officials, studied the country's customs records and commerce, observed the consular and diplomatic practice, Hodgson departed Egypt in early November. He traveled to Malta and there submitted a third report to the Secretary of State. He compared the agricultural production of Egypt to that of an American plantation in the cotton-South. He wrote that the country is a land of striking contrasts. On the one hand, there is great agricultural wealth based on a very fertile soil. On the other hand, there is a "miserably clothed peasantry," who till the soil but receive little compensation for their labor. They are miserably clothed, housed, and fed. They work the soil and the Pacha receives "the fruit of their labor, leaving to the unfortunate Arab the least possible means of subsistence." This wage amounted to about four cents per day. Egypt had four million acres of arable land and a population of some 2.5 million inhabitants. Hodgson described Muhammad Ali as the "lord, both of the land and the fellah. He is the sole great farmer and merchant; he collects his crops, transports them to Alexandria, and there sells them to Frank merchants, or ships them on his own accord to Europe." He related that the Pacha had embarked on his annual tour of inspection just prior to his (Hodgson's) return to Alexandria. While overseeing the planting of seed in the Delta during the winter months, the court of consular officials resided at Cairo to be near the Pacha. Concerning the ever-changing military situation in the Middle East, Hodgson observed that the Pacha's fleet had returned to Alexandria after a cruise off the Syrian coast. Ibrahim was at Damascus recruiting an army. At that time, a force of 12,000 men under Achmet Pacha, nephew of Muhammad Ali, was marching upon Yemen to compel the Imam of Sana, who possessed Mocha and the rich coffee country, to submit to the Egyptian overlord. With the completion of the expedition, Muhammad Ali would then be in possession of the rich coffee lands. With respect to commercial opportunity, Hodgson recounted his conversation with a Genoese merchant who told him that he was recently at Mocha, where he observed an American merchantship of four hundred tons lying there to take on a cargo of coffee. He noted that American ships annually brought about four cargoes of Mocha coffee direct to the Mediterranean and realized a profit of 120 percent.[15]

Because of heavy weather, Hodgson was delayed at Malta. He could have embarked on a small schooner of 80 tons for the winter trip across the Atlantic, but being a poor sailor, he declined to take passage. Writing to John Forsyth, he begged the Secretary to understand his reluctance to sail, saying "the coast of America in the winter season is sufficiently dangerous, even for large vessels. I shall have no doubt of finding a safer conveyance from the port of Gibraltar."[16] He used his time to prepare a preliminary report on his mission. Inasmuch as the report supplemented his earlier reports, I have abstracted a portion of it. The United States and Egypt, Hodgson observed, produced food stuffs and fiber of a similar nature, with cotton, rice, grain, and sugar being crops that would preclude a trade in these items. But he observed that there is a great variety of products in Egypt that the United States currently obtained by direct trade that might form the basis of direct commercial intercourse with Alexandria. Opium fell into this category, for Egypt then produced some 100,000 pounds per year. Some Americans, Hodgson pointed out, had already entered the Egyptian opium trade. Hypothetically, American merchants might like to import such products as gum arabic, incense, myrrh, and henna--articles of small bulk which would command a high price and offer a handsome return. There also were a number of items of large bulk and small profit that could be carried to American ports, such as salt, saltpetre, flax seed, flax, linen, dates, sesame, and ostrich feathers. He declared that the winter season is the ideal time to trade in Egypt, for the Arabs bring their products to market on the flood of the Nile. The government exacts no duties on exports, but places an ad valorem duty of three percent on imports in accordance with the Turco-American Treaty of 1830. While sales were on a cash basis, credit could be obtained. Suggesting a possible cargo emanating from an American port for Egypt, Hodgson listed coal, tar, pitch, rosin, turpentine, rum, tobacco, salted fish, timber, salt beef, pepper, pimento, cloves, candles, tea, cotton textiles, copper, lead, iron, whale oil, barrel staves, oars and spars, and other goods related to naval construction. Hodgson concluded his report with miscellaneous remarks about Egyptian money, weights and measures, and rates of exchange.[17]

Hodgson departed Malta in early 1835, traveled to Gibraltar and took passage for the United States. Arriving in late February, he promptly filed his report on 2 March 1835. With respect to Muhammad Ali's status, Hodgson reiterated that the Egyptian had for many years exercised some of the attributes of sovereignty. But between his 1805-appointment as Viceroy of Egypt and his war with the Sultan, he owed fealty to the Ottoman overlord. As such he paid an annual subsidy to the Sultan's treasury. Yet, he had never asserted his independence and still acknowledged himself to be the Sultan's vassal. He no longer paid tribute. His present state was that of de facto independence and nominal subjection. In the current state of relations, he had neither negotiated treaties with other states, nor made commercial ties with any, distinct from those already existing with the Porte. He had concluded an agreement with Britain to regulate commerce and transit across the land between Suez and Cairo which would soon carry a railroad over which British traffic to and from India would travel. Both England and France supported an independent Egypt, a condition consonant with their national interests. (This condition would change with the Convention of 1840 which would restore Egypt to Ottoman hegemony).

The second topic of Hodgson's lengthy report concerned the activities of the consulates in Egypt and current diplomatic usage. Hodgson wrote that Colonels Campbell and DuHamel, respectively the British and Russian consuls general, had furnished him much information that had been supplemented by Boghos Bey, the Egyptian Minister of Foreign Affairs. Hodgson exhibited a considerable knowledge of the subject. He observed that European consuls present in Egypt continued to present berats, letters accepting credentials and recognizing the bearer as a duly authorized consular official to the Pacha. These had been issued by the Sublime Porte. He listed the various consulates in Egypt and proceeded to outline the organization of that of Great Britain, explaining that it was the most efficient and best organized of the lot. No doubt chagrined that the Jackson administration had discontinued the practice of employing language students in its overseas posts, Hodgson observed that the French, Russian, Austrian, and Sardinian consulates did employ students to pursue a knowledge of Oriental languages. What is more important, he declared that the European Powers continued to maintain a connection between their consuls in Egypt and their ambassadors near the Sublime Porte. But he pointed out that the latter continued to follow the Pacha, who held his court at Cairo in winter and at Alexandria in summer. Although Egypt continued to recognize the right of extraterritoriality granted by the treaties with the Sublime Porte, Hodgson asserted that the Pacha desired to regulate the administration of justice and hoped to adopt the Code Napoleon to that end. That there were already mixed tribunals, consisting of Muslims and Franks, in operation in Cairo was evidence of the intention of the Egyptian leader.

In the third phase of his report, Hodgson addressed himself to a description of Egyptian commerce and industry and the nature and extent of foreign trade. That the science of statistics had not as yet been perfected in Egypt made it impossible for him to give the value of imports and exports in that country, and he cautioned that his figures were only an approximation. He supplied a list of nations carrying on extensive import-export trade with Egypt, with Turkey leading with a total of $6 million, followed by Austria with $3.7 million, and Britain with $2 million. These figures were for the year 1832, and they did not include the United States, because American trade with Egypt was of an indirect nature. During the last six months the United States had done a nice trade with countries bordering the Red Sea, but it was still relatively unimportant. During the first half of 1833 some 634 foreign vessels visited Egyptian ports. Of that number, Greece led with 228, followed by Austria with 153, Britain with 64, and

and France with 57. Hodgson noted that Egypt had no
shipping of her own, beyond a number of small vessels
engaged in coastal trade. He advised that trade with
Egypt was based on the treaties that the various nations had made with Turkey, and that commerce with
that country was unrestricted except for a three percent tariff. Inasmuch as the tariff was subject to
negotiation, and since the United States had not as
yet negotiated a tariff with Turkey, American goods
were subject to the French scale of evaluation. The
Pacha, Hodgson declared, respected all treaties between Turkey and other states. Finally, all nations
trading with the Sublime Porte were permitted to
trade in Egypt on the basis of perfect equality,
with no preferences given to any state. To establish
and extend commercial intercourse between Egypt and
the United States should be an objective of the State
Department. At present, he stated that American trade
with Egypt was only indirect, with American traders
carrying about one million dollars per year in coffee
cargoes via the Cape of Good Hope to Europe. Hodgson
asserted that the United States would not require a
treaty with Egypt unless Muhammad Ali declared his independence from Turkey. He concluded his report with
a strong argument for the establishment of an American
consul general in Egypt. Boghos Bey, he observed,
had advised him that the Pacha had a high opinion of
the United States and that it should send a consul
general to Egypt, for Mr. Gliddon's grade was very
low indeed. Hodgson suggested that the consul general in Egypt would have control over all consuls
and vice consuls in his jurisdiction and command a
salary of $3,000.00 per year. He should be assisted
by a secretary, who would also serve as a language
student. The secretary would be chosen from the ranks
of a college-educated body, thus ruling out nepotism.
Mr. Gliddon, he concluded, had represented the United
States for many years, but his being subject to British jurisdiction reduced his effectiveness.[18]

What can be said of Hodgson's mission to Egypt?
The United States did elevate the rank of its consular

agent at Alexandria to consul. With Commodore Porter strongly in favor of Gliddon, the latter received the appointment in March 1835. He held the post until his death in 1844, when his Scottish-born son-in-law succeeded him and held the position until 1848. It was not until that year that an American consulate general was created at Alexandria with a native son to fill that post. American trade did not greatly increase with Egypt during the years following Hodgson's mission.[19] Aside from the elevation of the American consular official at Alexandria, the only other material benefit that accrued from Hodgson's assignment was that his mission served as a model for later American diplomatic missions to the Middle East. Of course he did provide the Department of State with a wealth of data concerning Egyptian commercial and diplomatic practice.[20]

Given Hodgson's interest in language, one might well wonder why he left no record of his journey to Egypt, a land noted for its ancient monuments, many of them inscribed with the fascinating hieroglyphics. If Hodgson visited the pyramids, with their tombs full of the ancient writings, or the famous Temple at Karnak, he left no journal or diary to document such an experience. Undoubtedly, the secret nature of his visit precluded his keeping any such records even if he did journey to the famous monuments. But what is more to the point is that Hodgson simply did not have the time to visit the famous Egyptian pyramids and other antiquities.

Perhaps the most concrete result of Hodgson's mission to Egypt was his publication of a <u>Biographic Sketch of Muhammad Ali, Pacha of Egypt, Syria, and Arabia</u>, published by Peter Force in Washington in 1837. Comparing his subject to Napoleon Bonaparte, Hodgson traced the rise of Muhammad Ali from his humble beginning as a tobacco vender to the throne of an extensive empire. He extolled the virtues of this Egyptian who aspired to raise Egypt to the level of European civilization. Hodgson pointed out that the Egyptian leader had given patronage to the arts and sciences, had encouraged the migration of Europeans of talent, had founded schools at the elementary and technical level, and had been responsible for the opening of factories and the accomplishment of numerous internal improvements.[21] That Hodgson was able to meet and chronicle the Egyptian who is regarded as the founder of modern Egypt is interesting, and, undoubtedly his Sketch provided Americans with their first insight into an important historical figure.

By the time of the 1837 publication of this sketch, Hodgson had undertaken two important missions for the Department of State. It is now appropriate to take a look at his assignments to Tangier and Peru.

# 6
# WASHINGTON INTERLUDE

Chapter 6

A Washington Interlude

with

Missions to Morocco, Peru, and Germany

Hodgson's return to the United States in the Spring of 1835 found the nation riding a high tide of prosperity. President Jackson's removal of funds from the United States Bank and distribution to the "Pet Banks" brought on speculation in the West, where bankers indulged in a long-suppressed desire to gamble on western lands. New state banks were chartered, and there was a marked upturn in inflation as more loans were issued to sate the desire to speculate on land. There was also a sense of financial uncertainty in the country, for there was a shortage of funds in the mercantile Northeast. But the West thrived as never before on land sales, and it was during this time that the phrase "doing a land-office business" entered the American language. Although the Compromise Tariff of 1833 had provided for a scaling-down of rates that brought on reduced tariff receipts in the U.S. Treasury, nevertheless land sales embarrassed the Treasury, which was able to pay off the last vestige of the public debt in 1835.

Although prosperity and optimism reigned in the financial sphere, there was difficulty in the political arena, for the nullification controversy, spawned by the fertile mind of John C. Calhoun, the political genius from South Carolina, and the President's war on the U.S. Bank split the Democratic Party. The National Republican opponents of Jackson soon referred to themselves as Whigs who had little in common except their antipathy for "King Andrew I." The Whig Party encompassed a wide spectrum of political thought that included National Republican supporters of Henry Clay's American System, manufacturers who argued strongly for a high tariff, and anti-Jackson, state-rights Southerners. To the Whigs drifted Henry Clay, Daniel Webster, and Hodgson's old benefactor, Judge McLean, who was nominated for the presidency by the Ohio legislature in 1836.

But if Hodgson in the mid-1830s had lost his main political connection through John McLean, who was out of favor with the Jacksonians, he was soon to have a more able, more powerful benefactor in Martin Van Buren, Jackson's chosen successor, who would be elected to the presidency in 1836. But that was one year later. In 1835, we can infer from a letter from Hodgson to John Forsyth that the former was not then employed at the State Department. He noted that he had lost his clerkship when he accepted the post of interpreter at Constantinople.[1] Undoubtedly, Hodgson must have been somewhat pessimistic about his future in the closing years of Jackson's tenure in the White House.

It must have come as a pleasant surprise to Hodgson when Secretary of State John Forsyth appointed him as a Special Agent to go to Tangier to offer presents to the Emperor of Morocco upon the renewal of the Treaty Amity and Commerce between the United States and Morocco.[2] He ordered Hodgson to proceed immediately to New York, there to board the <u>U.S.S. Constitution</u> for Tangier. His instructions called for him to pick up the presents in New York. In addition to delivering the presents, Hodgson was also to deliver dispatches to James R. Leib, the U.S. Consul at Tangier. Unless retained at Tangier by Leib, Hodgson was directed to obtain the first available transportation and return to the United States with the renewed treaty.

Morocco was the first of the Barbary states to negotiate a treaty with the United States. Since the negotiation of this treaty in 1786, American trade with Morocco had not materialized. Nevertheless, the Jacksonians were anxious to expand American commerce on all fronts and found it desirable to renew this treaty at the expiration of its fiftieth year for an additional fifty-year period. Although piracy no longer complicated the negotiations, Anglo-French colonial aspirations were a factor in the Moroccan question in the 1830s. French imperialistic ambitions in Africa were whetted with the invasion of Algiers in 1830. The French were suspected by the British and Americans of further ambitions in Morocco. Lord Palmerston, British Foreign Minister between 1830 and 1841, established British policy vis-à-vis Morocco. Morocco would remain free to provide British merchants with commercial opportunity, to provide British needs for food supplies in the Mediterranean, and to ensure that no foreign power obtained a lodgement from which to threaten the British route to India. Since the United States also desired to further commerce with Morocco, Britain could hope to count on Yankee support in Morocco. But American trade with Morocco had not reached anticipated expectations, for Americans were preoccupied with expansion to the West. In 1835 American attention had turned to Texas, where there was a rumbling of discontent among Texans who could not accept the increased restrictions placed upon them by the distant government in Mexico City. In spite of the growing spirit of Manifest Destiny which would impel Americans to annex Texas and Oregon in the coming decade and then add California in its mission to establish a continental empire, Jacksonians were determined to preserve treaty rights with Morocco. In 1833

American Consul Leib had journeyed to Fez with the objective of applying for the renewal of the Treaty of 1786. Sultan Abd er-Rahman gave his word that the treaty would be renewed on receipt of a special letter from President Jackson or a special commission for negotiations. Accordingly, Hodgson was instructed to carry to Leib a special commission or letter of credence to negotiate the renewal.[3]

Hodgson departed Washington for New York on 11 August, and the journal that he kept on his mission to Tangier indicates that his stay was not without its interesting moments.[4] In New York Hodgson accepted delivery of the presents, a miscellany of objects that included a large inscribed mirror, three paintings, a writing desk and pen, a sword and some medals.[5] The gifts safely stowed aboard the Constitution, Hodgson settled down for an uneventful, twenty-three day voyage to Tangier. Arriving at the Moroccan port and finding that Mr. Leib was absent at Cadiz, Spain, the Constitution sailed for Gibraltar to await further instructions. Hodgson spent an enjoyable stay at the British bastion on the western approach to the Mediterranean. His journal leaves an interesting comment on his social life that reveals something of his character. Having received word from Leib that he was to remain at Gibraltar, Hodgson made the most of his opportunity. In addition to visiting Algeciras in Spain, Hodgson dined with Major General Sir Alex Woodford, the British governor of the fortress-rock. As the guest of honor, he was seated to the right of Lady Woodford, who told him that his English was very good, meaning, as Hodgson wrote, that "I had some of the conventional phrases and intonations of English society." He also records that he attended a bull fight at San Roque, and he described a rather gory ordeal that included the tumultous ovation that accompanied the dispatch of the "unfortunate, bloody bull." His social life also included dinners with other British military and diplomatic figures whose company he seems to have enjoyed. This interesting vignette provided by his journal portrays a young American whose character included the ambivalent admiration of British society and social customs, along with the republicanism that had taken root in the United States.

Hodgson's brief respite from his duties was cut short by receipt of instructions calling for him to sail to Tangier. Arriving on 7 October after a short, but rather stormy cruise, he repaired at once to the house of James Leib. Leib had already advised the State Department of Hodgson's safe arrival. He disclosed that the renewal of the treaty could not be effected in the near future and would probably require further negotiation. Concerning Hodgson, he wrote: "At the present moment, it is impossible to say for what period the detention of Mr. Hodgson may be expedient, but I am desirous of availing myself of his knowledge of the Arabic in the supervision of the necessary correspondence." He advised that negotiations would go forward in the utmost secrecy, because the European Powers would employ all efforts to hinder their conclusion.[6]

Secrecy was indeed necessary, for the British and French suspected that the United States had ulterior designs in Morocco. Although Washington merely desired to renew the treaty to safeguard future commercial opportunities, Luella Hall claims that British and French officials, including the lofty Lord Palmerston, British Foreign Secretary, and the stolid Louis Thiers, French Minister of Foreign Affairs, were concerned about the thrust of Hodgson's mission.[7]

But Hodgson's assignment in Tangier included nothing more than the treaty renewal, and he entertained no thoughts of imperialism, but was content simply to make himself useful to Leib in order that his career might not suffer. A letter to the Secretary of State expressed Hodgson's hopes for the mission. He wrote that he was quite willing to remain at Tangier, where his "experience and knowledge of Barbary manners and Moorish diplomacy" should prove valuable in treating with the government of Morocco. He asserted that he was quite prepared to act as "Arabic interpreter for any contingencies which this mission might present."[8] Shortly after arriving at Tangier, Hodgson was exceedingly happy to fulfill Leib's hopes for him by an early demonstration of his knowledge of Arabic. After settling in at Leib's residence, the Moroccan Deputy Collector of Customs arrived. In the presence of Leib, Hodgson exchanged compliments with the official, as is the custom in the East. The latter exclaimed at the American's knowledge of Oriental customs and the Arabic language, whereupon Hodgson replied that he "had long lived among Muslims." Leib explained to the Moroccan that Hodgson had served at the American Legation at Constantinople and in Algiers but he declined to reveal any details about Hodgson's mission, the better to preserve secrecy.[9] So impressed was Leib of Hodgson's performance that he reiterated to Forsyth his confidence in him, saying that he had already rendered valuable service and that he desired to retain him "under the title of Arabic Secretary to the Legation." He concluded that Hodgson found the arrangement perfectly satisfactory.[10]

But the negotiations went forward slowly, and Hodgson soon found that he had much time on his hands. After having turned over his cargo of presents to Leib's safekeeping, Hodgson used his leisure time to visit the members of the consular corps, whose beautiful residences impressed him. While visiting the home of one of the consuls, Hodgson witnessed an Arab wedding. He also had an occasion to visit several Jewish families in Tangier, a town that could boast a large Jewish community. He attended a synagogue where Leib's charity during the late cholera epidemic was extolled. He also amused himself in a dalliance with a young Muslim woman who told him that if she were suspected of being in love with a Christian, she would lose her head. On one occasion he had a long conversation with a learned Muslim who discussed trigonometry and geometry with him.[11] Moving from the sublime to the ridiculous,

Hodgson recorded in his journal that one afternoon he hurriedly arrived at a certain consul's residence which afforded him a vantage point from which to view a rather bizarre spectacle. It seems that a large group of Bedouin tribesmen, led by their sheiks, had come to town. Their assemblage was preceded by banners whipping in the breeze, and its members marched to the strident cadence of drums. The nomads danced before their sheikhs "in perfect order jumping into the air and throwing their heads backward and forward facing the sheikhs, of whom there were six or seven." To observe their "carniverous power," Hodgson purchased a young goat, had its throat cut, and placed out in the street. In short order a group of twenty or more leaped on the body of the goat "very much like a pack of hounds upon a fox." They tore open the belly of the animal and tossed its entrails into the air. Soon the hands and faces of the tribesmen were besmirched with blood.[12]

But Hodgson's time was not wholly devoted to leisurely pursuits, for his expertise with Arabic was soon put to use. On 24 October he wrote a letter to the authorities of the Emperor, asserting that the President desired to renew the treaty of 1786. The President, Hodgson explained, had sent him out with a special commission, duly empowering the American Consul to treat. He and the taleb employed by the Legation spent much time dickering over the proper wording of the missive. The letter enclosed an Arabic translation of the special commission brought by Hodgson to Leib, authorizing the latter to negotiate the treaty renewal.[13]

Subsequently, Hodgson informed Forsyth that he had been of service during the negotiations in his capacity of Arabic Secretary. It must have given Hodgson real satisfaction to extol his own value in such a self-congratulatory manner, for he was only too aware that Forsyth knew of the circumstances which had compelled the Department to remove him from Constantinople. Hodgson noted that the writing of the letter to the Emperor's Foreign Minister was quite involved, because "Morocco is the only state in Barbary where diplomatic negotiation is conducted in writing." He advised that he had translated several letters into Arabic and that these had been posted to the Emperor, who was then at the city of Morocco (Marrakech), one of the capital cities of the nation. The Emperor had replied that Mr. Leib could begin talks with his representative in Tangier.[14] On 28 November, Leib, accompanied by Hodgson, had an audience with the Kaid Elabi Espaidi who assured him that the Emperor would place his seal on the treaty and that it would be posted from Morocco about 1 January.[15]

The talks concluded, Leib wrote the Secretary that Hodgson's service was no longer needed, that he would shortly return to Washington bearing a journal of the negotiations had with the Emperor's government, and that he hoped he would also bear the renewed treaty.[16] However, as events unfolded, Hodgson did not return the renewed treaty to the United States. The Treaty of 1836 was not signed until 16 September 1836, some seven months after Hodgson's departure for Washington. Luella Hall suggests that the negotiations dragged on by correspondence during 1836, hence the delay in bringing them to fruition while Hodgson was still in Morocco. She alludes to the possibility that the British and French, suspicious of American intentions, might well have taken steps to delay completion of the negotiations.[17]

Although Hodgson could take pride in his assistance to Leib in moving the negotiations forward, he nevertheless expressed no little concern to the Secretary about his future with the State Department. It would appear that his prospects were quite dim, as he admitted to Forsyth, and that he wished to return to Washington to make application for further employment with the Department.[18]

Nevertheless, before departing from Morocco, Hodgson found the time to make a journey on horseback to the city of Tetuan. En route, he saw numerous Arabs riding camels headed for market with their flocks. His overland journey carried him from the cool seacoast, through a hot, arid desert, and over a high, cool mountain. At Tetuan Hodgson was met by several Moorish dignitaries, and the Bashaw presented him with the key to his city. Hodgson returned to Tangier about mid-November. His journal does not relate the extent of his activities between then and his departure for the United States on 17 February 1836. We can assume that he arrived in the United States in April.

His arrival in Washington held out little immediate hope for future employment. In December he wrote the Secretary of State, requesting reappointment to the clerkship which he relinquished when he accepted the position of interpreter at Constantinople. "Having been deprived of that place," Hodgson pleaded that he "would be most happy to return to employment in the Department of State."[19] I have not been able to determine whether Hodgson obtained his clerkship. At all events, in January 1837 he applied to the Secretary for a post that had fallen vacant in the consulate at Tangier. Although his application was supported by numerous members of the Virginia delegation to Congress, Hodgson did not receive the post.[20] Undismayed, he applied to President Jackson in March, pointing out that Congress had created two missions to Prussia and Austria, with each being supported by a secretary of legation. Hodgson requested one of the secretaryships, either at Berlin or Vienna. He asserted that his knowledge of French and German would make him of considerable value to the minister.[21] In spite of his linguistic expertise and his past experience, Hodgson was again disappointed. Undaunted, he applied in June for a position as translator in the Department. I have been unable to determine whether he received the post, but one of his letters of endorsement indicated that although Hodgson then resided in Washington, he was a frequent visitor to Richmond, where he visited the well-known newspaper editor and friend of Andrew Jackson, Thomas Richie. An examination of Richie's manuscript collection at the Library of Congress did not disclose any written contact between Hodgson and the newspaperman.

During the time of his unemployment, Hodgson kept his hand busy in the study of Oriental languages, and he also maintained contact with those who shared his interest. In May, 1836, Hodgson presented to the University of Virginia a part of the Gospel of St. Luke translated into the Berber language.[23] Hodgson's interest in the American Philosophical Society continued, and in April, 1835, he presented to Peter S. Duponceau a collection of Middle Eastern coins from Turkey, Egypt, and Greece.[24] He also donated to the Society a translation of the Lord's Prayer, made by Abderrahman. This Muslim had been abducted late in the 18th century and carried into slavery. For some forty years he remained in slavery near Natchez, Mississippi. While the translation is not literal, it was, as Hodgson described it, a Muslim version written in Mauretanic characters.[25] In 1837 he published in the Journal of the Royal Asiatic Society a translation of a travel account, originally written at his direction by a native speaker of the Berber dialect of Morocco.[26]

Shortly after presenting the translation of the Lord's Prayer to the American Philosophical Society, Hodgson received orders from Secretary of State John Forsyth, instructing him to journey to Peru to deliver dispatches to James E. Thornton, the American Chargé d'Affaires at Lima, and to place in his hands the ratified Treaty of Peace, Friendship, Commerce, and Navigation made by the United States with the Confederation of Peru and Bolivia. Hodgson was ordered to exchange the ratification with the proper authorities and return to the United States with the ratified copy of the treaty and such dispatches as the American Chargé might place in his care.[27] Hodgson promptly departed Washington on 15 October 1837 and traveled via Philadelphia to New York. Following a two week stay in the latter city, he sailed for Kingston, Jamaica on the packetship J.W. Cater on 1 November.[28] Hodgson's journal of his voyage and mission indicates that it was not without incident. He arrived at Kingston on 14 November, and there took a small boat to overtake the Henrietta, a schooner bound for Chargres, Panama. The small boat was upset in the ocean, and a Spanish schooner picked Hodgson up and carried him to Port Royal just a few miles from Kingston. Having purchased dry clothes and other supplies for his voyage, Hodgson took passage on the Countess of Mulgrave, a cattle carrier, bound for Cartegena on the Caribbean coast of Colombia. The weather was pleasant, but Hodgson was disgusted with the odors associated with the cattle boat. He arrived at the Colombian port on 28 November and promptly went ashore to see the American consul and to book passage for the voyage to Panama. Following visits to the various members of the consular corps, Hodgson sailed on 6 December on the Dolorita, captained by José Maria Medina, a black sailor, whom Hodgson described as having no "science of navigation, no quadrant, no compass, and a Spanish chart dated 1808." Medina sailed close to the coast, and Hodgson soon found himself quite seasick as the small vessel made her way through the incessant groundswells. Hodgson must have been happy to arrive at Portobelo, Panama ten days later. Following a two-day stay at Portobelo at which he attended a ball, where whites and blacks co-mingled on the dance floor, Hodgson took passage on a small vessel bound for Chargres. From Chargres he set out with a guide on an overland journey across the isthmus for Panama which he reached on 23 December. Along the way he saw crocodiles and numerous snakes, heard the constant chatter of parrots, and endured a heavy rainshower. While awaiting the arrival of his baggage at Panama, Hodgson found the time to attend a cockfight with the American consul on Christmas Eve. However, the inclement weather and the difficult conditions of travel had taken their toll, for Hodgson's health failed. On 18 January he placed the treaty in the hands of a Dr. Evans of Albany, New York who would convey it to Lima and deliver it to the American Chargé.[19]

Convalescing at Panama until 1 February, Hodgson regained his health. He embarked on the U.S.S. Enterprise and on 5 February sailed for Peru. One of his fellow passengers was Peruvian, and he filled Hodgson in on the details of the Peruvian-Bolivian Confederation. Peru gained its independence on 15 July 1821, while Bolivia, known as Upper Peru, proclaimed its independence in 1825. The Confederation of Peru and Bolivia was formed in 1836, and a treaty was made with the United States. It was this treaty that Hodgson was instructed to bear to Lima to exchange ratifications with the proper authorities of the Confederation.

Hodgson arrived at the Peruvian port of Callao on 27 March and dined with Captain Isaac McKeever on board the U.S.S. Falmouth. It was at this time that he learned that James B. Thornton, the Chargé to whom he was to deliver the treaty and dispatches, had died, and Hodgson duly reported to Edwin Bartlett, the American Consul at Lima.[30] He then advised the Secretary of his arrival at Callao, disclosing that although complications had arisen, he had high hopes of completing his mission and would comply with the instructions of Bartlett.[31] The complication that Hodgson referred to in his letter was the death of the American consul James Thornton on 25 January. His successor, Edwin Bartlett, informed Forsyth that Hodgson had arrived with the treaty and dispatches and that all was in good order. He had called on the Minister of Foreign Affairs at Lima to make the exchange of ratifications, but this would require special permission from General Andrew Santa Cruz, the Protector of the Confederation. He advised that he had ordered Hodgson to proceed shortly on the Falmouth to Islay and then on to LaPaz, there to obtain the needed permission from the Protector for the exchange.[32]

While awaiting the departure of the Falmouth, Hodgson enjoyed a constant round of entertainment with the members of the consular corps. His journal, written in Spanish in part, indicates his liking for the British consul general and demonstrates a working knowledge of Spanish. There was a delay in the sailing of the Falmouth, for, although the Captain had received instructions from Bartlett to proceed with Hodgson to one of the South Peruvian ports (Islay or Arica), the ship did not sail until somewhat later. Captain McKeever was of the opinion that he should await the arrival of Commodore Henry Ballard, the senior American naval officer in Pacific waters adjacent to South America, at Callao before proceeding.[33]

Ultimately, the Falmouth sailed, carrying Hodgson, who was accompanied by Colonel José Romera, a Peruvian commissioner, and she arrived at the port of Islay about midnight on 25 April. Hodgson and his companion spent the night in the residence of the military commandant, but on the following day set out by muleback for Arequipa, where they arrived late in the evening. Hodgson's journal indicates that he found the journey fatiguing, for he and his companion agreed to pass some time in Arequipa to recoup their strength. During the stopover, Hodgson took the opportunity to visit the local prefect, who entertained him. We can assume that he was utilizing the delay to recover from the uncomfortable travel on the back of a mule and to exercise his knowledge of Spanish. Hodgson and Colonel Romero set out with an English traveler on muleback on 1 May, bound for LaPaz. They ascended the Andes Mountains and Hodgson began to complain of discomfort.[34] His breathing was labored and accompanied by vomiting. Unable to proceed further into the mountains, Hodgson turned over his dispatches and the ratified treaty to Colonel Romera, who proceeded on with the English traveler. Hodgson returned slowly to Arequipa. There to his dismay, he learned that the Protector was absent from LaPaz and would not return until mid-June. He was visiting the city of Cochabamba on Confederation business, and this would require that the Colonel proceed further inland, thus causing further delay in completing the exchange of ratifications. Hodgson noted in his journal that he was not at all sanguine about the completion of his mission, for he learned that the Bolivian Congress would shortly determine the future of the Confederation at its June meeting.

Hodgson remained at Arequipa until 31 May. Having received no word from Colonel Romera, he determined to return to Callao. He sailed on the <u>Falmouth</u> on 1 June and arrived on the 9th. He was still at Callao when Colonel Romera arrived on the 30th without the ratified copy of the treaty. The Colonel related that the Protector had kept him at Cochabamba for eighteen days, resulting in an inordinant delay in completing the mission. It seems that Romera was unable to make the exchange by 30 May in accordance with Article 30 of the treaty. To remedy the situation, Bartlett called personally on Juan Garcia del Rio, a commissioner authorized by the Protector to exchange the ratifications, and there made the exchange in accordance with the strict letter of the treaty.[35] Bartlett so advised the Secretary of State. In due course he delivered the ratified treaty to Hodgson and released him to return with it to the United States.

While the trip to the snowcapped Andes must have been interesting to Hodgson, who had spent much of his foreign service career in the flat, hot, sandy regions of the Middle East, it nevertheless took its toll. Bartlett's letter to Forsyth indicates that Hodgson was not in good health. But the remainder of his stay at Callao gave him time to recuperate from the rigors of his travel.

He remained at the Peruvian port until mid-July. But in addition to rest and recreation, Hodgson had an altercation with Commodore Henry Ballard, U. S. Navy, Commander of the Pacific Squadron. It seems that Commodore Ballard accidentally broke the seal of a letter written by Hodgson and then read a few lines of the message before realizing his mistake. Ballard then ordered Hodgson to come aboard the U.S.S. North Carolina, flagship of the Pacific Squadron. Hodgson complied, and on being told that the letter had been opened, got involved in a heated exchange with the Commodore. Eventually, tempers cooled, and the two men shook hands on parting. But that was not the last of the matter, for in 1842 Hodgson preferred charges against Ballard, who was tried by a general court-martial on board the North Carolina in New York harbor. Among the officers sitting on the court were Commander Josiah Tattnall and Captains James Barron and James Biddle. The testimony given at the court-martial was long and rambling. Hodgson's counsel charged that Ballard not only opened and read the letter, but that he also was abusive toward Hodgson. The Commodore's defense was built on the premise that his eyesight was impaired, that the cabin was dark, and that his opening of the letter was "casual" and "accidental." The court found Ballard guilty of "conduct unbecoming an officer and a gentleman," and sentenced him to suspension of all pay and allowances for one year, as of 12 September 1842.[36]

The untoward incident leading to the court-martial occurred on the evening before Hodgson departed Callao for the United States. With the ratified treaty and dispatches in his possession, Hodgson sailed on the U.S.S. Lexington for Panama on 14 July. He arrived on 25 July and remained there until such time as he could obtain passage for Jamaica. While at Panama, Hodgson became involved in another incident. It seems that a certain Captain Glendy insulted him. I can only infer that Glendy was the commanding officer of the Lexington, which had conveyed Hodgson from Callao to Panama. Hodgson claims that Glendy insulted him on his ship, and that when he sent the naval officer a request to obtain satisfaction by an "appeal to arms," the officer refused. Hodgson described Glendy as a "brute who was too cowardly to fight." However, the officer did offer Hodgson an apology.[37]

Hodgson departed Panama on 20 August, traveling overland to Chagres. His trip was a hard one which he described as being made under torrential rains amidst swarms of mosquitos. He sailed for Kingston on 29 August, arriving on 8 September. At this point Hodgson concluded his journal on a somber note. He lamented that he would not reach Washington until late October and that he had little promise for future employment by the Department of State.[38]

There is one interesting comment that must be made on Hodgson's journal. Although not trained as a geographer, he did make numerous notes about the Isthmus of Panama. He observed that it was the ideal location for a future canal connecting the Atlantic and Pacific. That the future builders would incur innumerable obstacles is patently clear from his journal entries on the terrain.

Hodgson returned to Washington in October. Although the cooler climate would have been welcome after spending such a long time in the tropics, he must have had misgivings about his future. His journal indicates that he was aware that his mission was for naught, for the Bolivian Congress had already decided to separate from Peru. Indeed, the Peruvian-Bolivian Confederation did come to an end in 1839, and the two states both went their separate ways.[39] He had little hope of employment outside of the government, for the country was then suffering from the adverse conditions that resulted from the Panic of 1837, one of the worst economic depressions yet experienced by the American people. Hodgson did have good connections with the administration of President Martin Van Buren. He knew him personally and he also knew his Secretary of State, John Forsyth. In April of the following year, Hodgson wrote Forsyth, requesting appointment to a clerkship in "your Department which I understand is vacant. If you should be pleased to make me your librarian, I would endeavor to serve you, with intelligence and devotion."[40] The position did not materialize.

Washington & Missions    117

However, the following year found Hodgson again employed by the Department of State. Secretary Forsyth instructed him to proceed to Berlin to deliver dispatches and a ratified treaty to Henry Wheaton, the American Envoy Extraordinary and Minister Plenipotentiary. Intrusted to his care was the Treaty of Commerce and Navigation between the United States and Hanover, signed at Berlin on 20 May 1840, and ratified by the President on 28 July 1840. Hodgson was instructed to return the copy of the treaty ratified by Hanover to the United States.[41]

Hodgson traveled promptly to New York, where he wrote the Secretary that he would sail on the Toronto for Britain on 10 August. His letter contained an application for the post of consul at Tangier in the event that a vacancy occurred.[42] Hodgson traveled via London, where he called on Andrew Stevenson, the American Minister to the Court of St. James. He arrived at Berlin in October. Wheaton, the American Minister, acknowledged Hodgson's arrival with the dispatches and treaty. He advised Forsyth that Hodgson would be detained for a short while in Berlin in order that some last minute details might be ironed out between the Hannoverian minister and himself. He advised that Hodgson would probably return to the United States about 1 November.[43] During the hiatus, Hodgson took the opportunity to travel in East Germany, visiting Dresden, Weimar, and Koenigsberg. While in Berlin he attended a ceremony in which the Prussian people paid hommage to Frederick William IV, the newly crowned monarch of Prussia. He found the spectacle inspiring, and confessed to Andrew Stevenson that "I have learned to appreciate the virtues of the German people."[44] Hodgson returned to England and sailed from South Hampton on the British Queen on 2 November, arriving in New York on the twentieth of that month.

The winter of 1840-1841 must have been a grim one for Hodgson. He was not only unemployed during a time of economic recession, but Martin Van Buren had been replaced at the White House by William Henry Harrison, the victor of the Battle of Tippecanoe. But Hodgson's old benefactor, Judge McLean, soon took up the younger man's cause with the newly elected Whig President. Writing to General Harrison on 10 March 1841, McLean reiterated Hodgson's past service to the nation in the Middle East. He recommended Hodgson as a man gifted in the use of Middle Eastern languages and suggested that he might be of further service to the country.[45] But within a month of his inauguration Harrison was dead. Hodgson wrote to McLean, admitting that the President's death gave him cause for concern about his future. But he exclaimed that Daniel Webster, the newly appointed Secretary of State, had assured him that he would be restored to his post as dragoman at Constantinople. Hodgson thanked McLean profusely for interceding with Webster on his behalf.[46]

Although Daniel Webster had little respect for Commodore Porter as the American Minister at Constantinople, he nevertheless had the good sense not to return Hodgson to the Ottoman capital, where the younger man would again have had to deal with the wily, bad-tempered, former naval person. Instead, Hodgson received an appointment later in the year that would place him at Tunis, far from his old nemesis on the Bosporus.

# 7
# AMERICAN CONSUL AT TUNIS

Chapter 7

American Consul at Tunis

Hodgson spent a long time in Washington in 1841, awaiting President John Tyler's decision on his future. He continued to hope for an appointment that would return him to Constantinople. But this did not materialize, for, as he wrote to his old patron, John McLean, the "ignorant position of a navy man has prevented me from fully accomplishing my own generous purposes and your own anticipations." Hodgson was of course referring to Commodore Porter's opposition to his appointment as dragoman at Constantinople. He advised McLean that the President would appoint him to a post either at Tunis or at Alexandria. He informed the older man that he would continue to "look to the East" to make his future. McLean must have been gratified to learn that the Asiatic Society of Paris had extended him recognition for a map of North Africa which he had submitted to the Society. Hodgson closed his letter on an optimistic note, relating that Secretary of State Daniel Webster had interviewed him and continued to maintain an interest in him.[1]

Hodgson's faith in Webster was not misplaced, for on 22 September 1842 he informed Hodgson that President Tyler had appointed him as Consul at Tunis to replace Samuel D. Heap, who was appointed as dragoman at the American Ministry at Constantinople. The letter included his Commission and a letter of credence to the Bey of Tunis. Webster ordered him to maintain amity and peace with the Bey, ensure that the treaty between the United States and Tunis was enforced in every respect, and suggested that he familiarize himself with the political affairs of the country. He added that Hodgson would find that his situation would permit him to further his study of Oriental languages. He urged him to transmit information of a political and geographical nature to the Department. Hodgson learned that his salary would be $2,000.00 per year and that he was to have a contingency fund of $800.00 per year. He was also allowed the sum of $3,000.00 for the purchase of presents for the Bey and those high officers and dignitaries closely associated with him.[2]

Hodgson had good cause to write McLean on his new appointment. He noted that Heap was the brother-in-law of Commodore Porter, and he bemoaned the fact that Porter continued to permit familial ties to influence his appointments. However, Hodgson continued to hope to return to Constantinople in the event that another vacancy existed. He was happy to have the new appointment, for Tunis was the most desirable post in the East next to Constantinople. The salubrious climate would agree with him. He advised that he would continue his studies of language, philosophy, history, and geography. He disclosed that he intended to correspond with the curators of the National Institution[3] about his work. He concluded his letter with words of thanks for McLean's willingness to act as his benefactor with the new administration, and he observed that "Mr. Webster has continued to be my fast friend, and I owe much to him for his unyielding support of me." Webster, he noted, would retain him as a linguist in the Department on a permanent basis following the termination of his service at Tunis.[4]

That Hodgson had been able to maintain a career with the Department of State during the time when diverse political leaders laid hold of the White House was a tribute both to his ability and to his luck. However, it was somewhat of a black mark against the American government, which continued to neglect taking those steps which would professionalize the body of men representing the American flag in overseas posts. While Hodgson could lay claim to expertise in European and Oriental languages, it seems safe to conclude that his continued employment by the Department of State depended as much on his acquaintance with persons high in the various administrations that held power in Washington as it did upon his special knowledge of languages.

Hodgson traveled from Washington to Boston, there to acquire the presents to be given to the Bey on his arrival in Tunis. While there he met Judge McLean's wife and son. He returned to New York to await passage for La Havre. He wrote McLean, asserting that he considered him to be his "first and best friend," but that he feared Commodore Porter would try to defeat his nomination as consul in the Senate. He divulged that Porter had influence with Senator Thomas Hart Benton who might try to stop his appointment. He noted that Porter had lodged charges at the Department of State, alleging that he (Hodgson) had been guilty of wrong-doing while at Constantinople. But he observed that Secretary of State Forsyth had heard and disposed of the charges and continued to repose good faith in him. He said that he had met Major Noah, a previous consul at Tunis who had given him much information about his new post.[5]

Hodgson also informed the State Department that he had purchased the necessary presents and that he hoped to reach France by 1 December. He related that he had heard that Britain and France were concentrating naval forces before Tunis. He stated that he was not yet sure of the intentions of the two European powers, but that it would appear that France wanted to bring the Regency of Tunis under its control, while Britain would endeavor to impede any such move.[6]

At this point, it is necessary to interject a note on the status of Tunis. France had achieved ascendancy over Algiers and the littoral of Algeria in 1830, but she had not moved into Tunis. The weakness of Tunis was obviously an enticement to the imperial-minded French. But France would not be able to overcome the opposition of Britain, which had adopted a policy to maintain the sovereignty of the small states on the Mediterranean littoral of Africa. Ultimately, in 1881 the French did occupy Tunis and establish a protectorate that lasted for three-quarters of a century.[7]

Hodgson sailed from New York City in early December. His winter crossing of the Atlantic was uneventful, and he arrived at La Havre little the worse for wear. Traveling to Paris, he delayed his journey for a short while for reasons that will be revealed later. Moving on to Marseilles, he booked passage for Tunis and arrived on 11 February, but only after a perilous transit of the storm-tossed Mediterranean. He arrived at the Goletta, the fortified port of Tunis about nine miles distant from the city. Guiseppe Gaspary, the U.S. Vice Consul, met him and conducted him to the city. Hodgson was welcomed with ceremony, for his approach to the old city was met by a show of flags from the staffs of all of the consulates. Shortly after his arrival, Hodgson received the various members of the consular corps in their official costume.[8]

The city of Tunis was the capital of one of the Barbary states whose pirates harassed American shipping during the previous century. The United States had enjoyed amicable relations with Tunis since Commodore Stephen Decatur pacified the Barbary states in 1816. By 1842 Tunis was greatly weakened, and several of the European Powers, notably Italy, Britain, and France maintained more than a passing interest in Tunis. In mid-century, Tunis enjoyed but a vestige of the power that it had displayed earlier in the century and in the days when the words "Barbary pirates" were a scourge to shippers on the Mediterranean. The city itself was in reality a medieval Arabic medina or metropolis. With its kasbah or fortress overlooking the maze of crooked streets and alleys and the innumerable covered markets or bazaars, it must have presented to Hodgson a wholly Oriental appearance. He was not long in having the opportunity of examining the old city.

On the 14th, Heap, the out-going consul, arranged for Hodgson to be presented to Ahmed Bey. Accompanied by Heap and one of the interpreters of the consulate, Hodgson proceeded in a coach to Bardo, a fortified town surrounded by a wall and ramparts located some two miles from Tunis. Signore Antonio Bozo, the Secretary for Foreign Affairs, conducted him to the reception salon and presented him to the Bey. Heap announced his transfer to Constantinople and Hodgson then delivered through the Secretary his letter of credence as consul. Hodgson expressed to the Bey the President's "friendly disposition" toward the maintenance of peace and amity. He announced that he had brought along some recently invented firearms which he would show to the Bey on the following day. Returning to Tunis, Hodgson and Heap called officially on the various members of the consular corps. Hodgson had the opportunity to meet the consuls of France, Britain, Sardinia, Naples, Holland, Spain, Sweden, and Belgium. Several of them he had met in other places in the Middle East.[9]

With the French conquest of Algiers, there developed a different relationship between the European Powers and those states of Barbary. No longer did the Europeans need to seek the good favor of Barbary heads of state by the presentation of gifts and tribute. Hodgson advised Daniel Webster that the conclusion of the treaty between France and Tunis in 1830 ended the giving of presents. Thus, the United States would not be compelled to distribute gifts to the Bey and to his officers. Hodgson advised that Heap suggested that the giving of the newly-invented American firearms would have a salutary effect upon relations between Tunis and the United States.[10] In a subsequent dispatch, Hodgson informed the Secretary that he had distributed a few articles of American manufacture, asserting that they would create a fund of good will for the administration of President Tyler. He observed that the distribution of favors would enable him to acquire a number of objects of this country for the National Institution in Washington. He hoped to acquire manuscripts, antiquities, and ancient coins.[11] With respect to the other presents, Hodgson and Heap signed a joint memorandum, advising that they would be returned to Malta to be sold at the highest price by W. W. Andrews, American consul at that place.[12]

Having disposed of the presents, Hodgson promptly presented to the State Department in obedience to his instructions an inventory of the books, papers, and property of the consulate. He noted that there was no letter book or record of dispatches from the consulate and that no journal of any sort had been maintained. He avowed that he would remedy this oversight.[13] Then in compliance with an interrogatory circular submitted by Secretary of State Webster to American consulates and ministries, Hodgson replied that the treaty existing between Tunis and the United States was being "faithfully executed and observed, that American commerce was receiving "uniform protection," that American merchants were trading in accordance with the most-favored-nation principle, and that it would be difficult to estimate the amount of American trade with Tunis.[14]

This was Hodgson's last official communication with the Secretary of State from Tunis, for he had determined to leave the consular service in order to get married. Leaving the affairs of the American consulate in the hands of W. R. B. Gale, the son of a New Orleans merchant, Hodgson departed Tunis in May and traveled via Malta and Naples to meet his affianced,

Miss Margaret Telfair, at Florence. There is a journal in the Hodgson papers that reveals some rather interesting facts about Hodgson and his anticipated marriage. En route, Hodgson stopped off at Malta. There he visited a British army mess. He recorded in his journal that he believed that the British Army "is the highest school of manners in the world." He admired the high birth of the officers and found them to be well educated and possessed of good breeding.[15] Filled with the republicanism of his time, Hodgson nevertheless had the profound admiration for the British that was found among many Americans born on the east coast. But given the reality that Hodgson was most probably living in Georgetown in 1814 when British troops marched into Washington and burned the executive mansion and other public buildings, one would think that Hodgson's anglophilia was somewhat pronounced. His journal also revealed that he had a keen desire to meet members of the Italian royalty and nobility. At Naples, the American Consul General arranged to have Hodgson presented to the King and Queen of Naples at a levee which Hodgson described in great detail.[16] He seems to have enjoyed his association with the high-born of Naples, but his journal also indicates that he was a man deeply in love.

Although at an age when most men are long past having the pangs of a first love, Hodgson's journal suggests that he was a man strongly attached to Margaret Telfair. He described her as a "gentle being who is the sole object of my thoughts." He looked forward to seeing her again in Florence, where she was enjoying the sights with her sister Mary.[17] Hodgson had made quite a catch for himself, for Margaret was a wealthy heiress. Her father was Edward Telfair, a wealthy Savannah merchant who had served in the Continental Congress from 1777 to 1783, was governor of Georgia for two terms, and left a large fortune to his daughters, Mary and Margaret. He had married Sally Gibbons in 1774 and by her had three sons and three daughters.[18]

We don't know much about the romance between Hodgson and Margaret, but he apparently met her in Paris in November, 1841, while en route to his post at Tunis. She had accepted his proposal of marriage, provided that he agree to resign from the consular service. He and Margaret had planned to marry in Switzerland, but since Swiss law required a residence of six months, they journeyed to London. On 3 July 1842 Hodgson submitted letters of resignation to President Tyler and to Secretary of State Daniel Webster. Hodgson wrote Tyler that a mere fifteen-day residence is required in London and that he would be married on 11 July 1842. Following the marriage, he said that he and his bride would make a tour of England, Ireland, and Scotland, and then return to the continent in the autumn. Hodgson hoped that the government would receive his resignation with good grace. Having been educated at government expense for special service in the field of foreign relations, he seems to have exhibited some qualms of guilt at leaving the service. Indeed, he concluded his letter to Webster, saying: "If the President should be pleased to call me again to that service, I will not decline the duty and the honor."[19]

Hodgson and Miss Telfair were duly married on 11 July 1842 in London at St. George's Church by the Very Reverend Robert Hodgson, dean of Carlisle Cathedral.[20] After a lengthy wedding trip, Hodgson and his bride arrived in Savannah late in 1842. They took up residence in the magnificent Telfair mansion, located on one of the city's many large squares. Although he would now find himself occupied with the administration of his wife's large estate, Hodgson nevertheless found it possible to continue to engage in scholarship, to travel frequently, and to maintain contact with the nation's leaders and with men who shared his interest in Oriental scholarship.

However, given Hodgson's marriage to a woman of great wealth and social position, the question inevitably arises: What future could Hodgson have enjoyed had he remained in the ranks of the nation's diplomatic representatives? Although members of the consular service seldom reached the ranks of the diplomatic corps during the nineteenth century, Hodgson had numerous assets that might well have enabled him to reach the position of minister. His experience in diplomatic usage, his knowledge of languages, his political connections, and his wife's wealth might well have provided him with the requisite qualifications to achieve ministerial rank, had he not been restricted by his wife's wishes.

# 8
# SAVANNAH
# AND
# SCHOLARLY ACTIVITIES

Chapter 8

Savannah and

Scholarly Activities

Upon his arrival in Savannah, Hodgson had already achieved eminence in the field of language study. His qualifications had earned for him membership in the American Philosophical Society, the Royal Asiatic Society, and the Société de Géographie of Paris. He had acquired a knowledge of Latin, Greek, German, French, modern Greek, Spanish, Arabic, Turkish, and Persian, not to mention Berber. He possessed a large and valuable collection of Oriental manuscripts and books. He easily fitted into the elect group of men who constituted Savannah's literary elite.

But Hodgson's reputation in scholarship extended far beyond the confines of Savannah. He had already made his mark in philology by his study of the Berber language. His publications in the <u>Transactions of the American Philosophical Society</u>, along with his <u>Notes of a Journey into the Interior of North Africa by Hadjii Ebn-ed-Din el Eghwaati</u> (London, 1830), a translation that he made from an Arabic travel sketch, and his successful efforts to translate parts of the Bible into a Berber dialect, had caused one writer to describe him as a "world pioneer" in the study of the Berber language.¹ Hodgson had earned the respect of scholars in both Great Britain and France, as well as in the United States. Dr. James Cowles Prichard, a British scholar, mastered and combined a study of zoological and philological ethnology in his book, Researches into the Physical History of Mankind, which contained a contemporary estimate of Hodgson's contributions.² Prichard acknowledged Hodgson's paper read before the American Philosophical Society in 1829, concluding that it contained "much valuable information on both subjects connected with the history of the Berbers," as well as a treatise on the Berber language. He noted that W. F. Newman, late Fellow of Balliol College and brother of the eminent Cardinal Newman, wrote a paper on the Berber grammar, relying solely on the portion of St. Luke's Gospel produced under Hodgson's guidance. The British scholar also credited Hodgson with supplying the scholarly world with an accurate description of the various Berber tribes.³

Hodgson's reputation had also spread to France. On 7 October 1836 he had been elected to membership in the exclusive and distinguised Société de Géographie of Paris.⁴ In 1838 he corresponded with M. D'Avezac, the Secretary General of the Société. Hodgson transmitted to the French scholar a Berber manuscript which contained a lengthy speciman of Berber writing, a description of Berber manners and customs, and some tales and songs. He also related to the Frenchman information about the relationship between the geography and the various languages as spoken by the tribes of North Africa. His letter of transmittal contained an interesting comment. Hodgson wrote: "Always deeply impressed with a sense of the high distinction conferred upon me by His Majesty, I should be greatly pleased if the present document or any others of the numerous papers which I possess should be found useful in the interest of the French colony at Algiers."⁵ I have not been able to determine exactly what "high distinction" Hodgson was referring to in his letter, but suffice it to say that King Louis Philippe took great interest in and gave his support to those engaged in the study of the arts and sciences. This bourgeois king's government consisted of the elites, those of birth, money, and intelligence, and he frequently honored those men whose achievements in scholarship pushed back the frontiers of knowledge.[6] What is so surprising is Hodgson's support of French colonialism, a pursuit diametrically opposed to the egalitarian principles of Jacksonian Democracy which he had so strongly espoused in the past.

But Hodgson had also worked in another area that placed him among those extending man's breadth of knowledge. His study of the peoples of Central Africa and their relation to the slave trade placed him in a premier place among those Americans who first evinced an interest in the origin of the African slave trade.[7] This is not at all surprising that a slave owner should find an interest in the origins of his African slaves, for we find that another Georgia slave owner, James Hamilton Couper, also inquired into the origins of his blacks. The vast majority of slaves in America had originated in the African Sudan. Medieval Muslims knew Africa south of the Sahara as the <u>Beled es-Sudan</u>, or "Land of the Blacks." Presently the term "Sudan" is used to describe the broad belt of grassland located south of the Sahara Desert and north of the tropical rain forest region that occupies the Guinea Coast and the Congo River Basin. The peoples who made up the chief source of the Negro population in the New World resided in the region of the western Sudan. The main area for the transatlantic slave trade was along the coast of West Africa between Senegal and Angola. Although some slaves came from deep in the interior, most of them came from the region that lies within three hundred miles of the coast. Having been taken captive by an African slave dealer, the slave would be carried to the coast and lodged in a barracoon until traded to an

American or European slave trader.[8] The "Middle Passage" across the Atlantic on a slaver could be a grueling trial to be endured by the slave. Graphically described by August Meier and Elliott Rudwick, this arduous journey, made in cramped quarters, generally lasted from forty to sixty days. Lodged in a 'tween deck area that measured some three feet ten inches on a Newport slaver, the voyage has been described as an ordeal. "It is not in the power of human imagination to picture to oneself a situation more dreadful or disgusting," wrote one observer.[9]

Hodgson, whose wife's estate included plantations that contained numerous slaves, initially addressed himself to a study of the Foulahs, a people who inhabited the Sudan. His study of this interesting people makes him one of America's first Sudanists, for his work on them is the first scientific work on any African people to be written by an American scholar.[10] His work on the Foulahs was published for the National Institute (later called the Smithsonian Institution) of Washington in 1843 under the title "The Foulahs of Central Africa and the Slave Trade." In this paper Hodgson concerned himself with some observations on the ethnography of Northern and Central Africa and considered the means by which the suppression of the Atlantic slave trade could be accomplished. He wrote that as early as 1831 he had begun to "regard Africa with much interest." He sought and read all books of travel, maps, scientific and medical works "that could give me any new ideas of Africa." Of particular interest to him was a people known as the Foulahs, or Fulani, as they are preferably called today. The Fulani, also variously known as the Fellani, Fellata, the Filani, Ful, Fulbe, Peul, and Pullo,[11] were described by Hodgson as a people who inhabited an area that extended from the Atlantic Ocean, at the mouth of the Senegal River, east to the Sahara reaches of the Sudan. He characterized them as a non-Negro people who "may be said to occupy the intermediate space betwixt the

Arab and the Negro." They are described as having a
"bronze, copper, reddish" color and regard themselves
as white men. They consider themselves among the
white nations." The Foulahs are a "warlike race of
shepherds" who subjugated a large portion of the Sudan. Hodgson observed that they were srict Muslims
and were indeed the missionaries of Islam among the
Negroes of Northern and Central Africa. As they
conquered with the sword, they forced upon the subject peoples the Koran. The Foulahs exercised an
enormous influence upon the moral and social conditions in Central Africa, and Hodgson concluded that
they could serve as an instrument to suppress the
slave trade on the Atlantic. He noted that he was
impressed with the moral superiority of the Foulahs,
a fact that he recorded in his 1830 article on this
subject in the Encyclopedia Americana. Hodgson regarded Christianity as a great civilizing force in
Africa, but viewed the Muslim faith as an even more
potent force in this respect. Together, the Koran
and the Gospel would serve "to bring up the civilization. . . ." He observed that the Koran prohibited
the enslavement of a "man born of free parents, and
professing the Muslim religion." Further, that no
Muslim could enslave another. He concluded his
essay with a speculative digression on the origins of
the Foulahs and with a brief discussion on the
origins of their language, saying that insufficient
evidence was available properly to investigate the
"Foulah tongue."[12]

Subsequent research on the Fulani has raised questions about Hodgson's conclusions concerning the non-
Negro racial characteristics of the Fulani, their warlike and pastoral occupations, and their fanatic ad-
herence to the Muslim faith. George Peter Murdock
tells us that some of the Fulani are strongly Negroid,
sedentary village dwellers, and not given to spreading
the Muslim faith by warlike means.[13] Further, he spec-
ulated on the linguistic and geographic origins of
these people, asserting that the Fulani originated in

the Atlantic subfamily of languages.[14]

Hodgson's association with those who shared his interest in the study of languages and people continued to be a main theme in his life, and in 1843 a new avenue for his scholarly pursuits opened up when he was elected to the American Oriental Society. This organization for the collection of knowledge relative to Oriental languages was founded in 1842 by John Pickering, the brilliant Boston attorney who devoted much of his life to the study of his own English language and those of the Oriental peoples as well.[15] Hodgson's letter acknowledging his election to the society indicated genuine satisfaction and pride and transmitted to the A. O. S. a copy of his paper on the Fulani.[16] In the following year, W. W. Greenough, corresponding secretary of the A. O. S., requested Hodgson to present a paper for inclusion in a volume of the society's transactions. Hodgson duly acknowledged the invitation, but declined due to previous commitments that included some African researches for the National Institute and for a newly organized commission, founded by the French government to initiate a study of the Berber language.[17] The society again honored Hodgson in 1846 with a request to address the membership at a meeting in Boston. Hodgson again declined, saying that he was spending the summer at Newport and had left all of his reference books and manuscripts at home in Savannah. He rationalized his refusal with the observation that "my mind is essentially practical, and demands in matters of science the most rigid facts. The preparation of a public discourse would therefore require time and the appliances which I have not now at command." He observed that he was then occupied with the study of some Georgia fossils that had recently come into his possession. He concluded with the reminder that he "took a lively interest in the success of our Society and nothing would give me greater pleasure than to be able hereafter to contribute a paper for the journal."[18] I cannot determine that Hodgson ever presented a paper to the membership of the A. O. S.

Although Hodgson and his wife passed the summers in fashionable Newport and spent the early autumn months in New York City, he nevertheless continued to maintain a vital interest in the study of Africa and the Middle East. While he had turned down two invitations to present papers to the American Oriental Society, he did give vent to his scholarly efforts elsewhere. He presented in 1844 a paper to the Ethnological Society of New York at its June meeting. Subsequently, he included his remarks in a slim volume, Notes on Northern Africa, the Sahara and Soudan, published in 1844 in New York by Wiley and Putnam.[19] Dedicated to Albert Gallatin, president of the New York society, this study contained an expanded version of his paper. At the outset, Hodgson reviewed the scholarship in the United States, Great Britain, France, and Germany pertinent to the study of the Berber language. Of course he did not fail to mention his own work. He then gave numerous examples of Berber words with their English equivalents. His study also included a number of Berber proverbs that "are almost identical with those in use among the most polished nations," and smack of the pithy wisdom of Benjamin Franklin. For example, he included:

> When the cat is out, the rats will play.
>
> Big fish devour the small.
>
> You are like one that strikes cold iron.
>
> Profit comes not from sleep.
>
> You are like the cock's feathers, waving with the wind.
>
> Speak not; the woods have ears.
>
> You are like one that pours water into a leaky tub.

Hodgson then launched into a discussion of the

Tuarycks, a nomadic people of the Sahara whose language is one of the Berber dialects. He remarked that he had transmitted to M. D'Avezac, Secretary General of the Société de Géographie of Paris, a manuscript volume of travels among the Tuarycks made by an educated taleb of Ghadamis. The work, commissioned by Hodgson while at Tunis, contained a "most detailed account of these nomads of the Sahara, their manners, customs, civil institutions, together with an Arabo-Tuaryck vocabulary." Hodgson noted that the Tuarycks were a white people of the Muslim faith.

Hodgson presented an extensive survey of North Africa, covering the exploits of the Medes and Persians, the Romans, the Germanic tribes, the Arabs, and the coming of the Ottoman Turks. He observed that the Berbers had inhabited the region during all this time. In fact, he asserted that the Mediterranean coast of Africa is called Barbary and its inhabitants are Barbars or Berbers. His historical analysis was followed by an extensive bibliography of materials related to the peoples of North Africa, their language, geography, and travel accounts of visitors to the region. His bibliography was coupled with a discussion of manuscripts related to the study of Berber.

Following a reproduction of his aforementioned essay on the Fulani, Hodgson included in his study a letter from James Hamilton Couper, the wealthy co-owner of Hopeton Plantation, which was located near Darien, Georgia. Couper related that there were about a dozen Negro slaves on his plantation who spoke and understood the Foulah language, even though they were not native Foulahs. For example, there was Tom, whose African name was Sali-bul-Ali, who had been purchased around 1800. His industry and intelligence had caused Couper to appoint him head driver of the plantation, with charge over about four hundred and fifty slaves. So dependable was Tom that Couper frequently left the plantation in his charge, without relying on the services of a white overseer. A strict Muslim, Tom abstained from alcohol and observed the various fasts, particularly that of Ramadan. Moreover, he could read Arabic and had a Koran in his possession. He did not write in Arabic. Couper provided Hodgson with a background for his head driver, based on the latter's African reminescences. Tom had been reared in Kianah, a Foulah colony in the Sudan. His people were Muslim and supported themselves by keeping large herds of horses, cows, sheep, and goats and by cultivating the soil. Their diet included rice, milk, fish, vegetables, beef, and mutton. They raised cotton from which they manufactured their own cotton cloth, and they also fashioned woolen blankets made from the long wool of their sheep. The native children learned to read and write Arabic. Tom's tale ended on a note of tragic irony, for, although his family had considerable property and had no slaves--slavery being forbidden by Koranic law--Tom was captured at the age of twelve and sold into slavery. Couper concluded his letter with a brief Foulah vocabulary.[20]

Hodgson related that Thomas Spalding, the statesman, business man, leading agriculturist, and the owner of a well known and prosperous plantation on Sapelo Island, one of Georgia's Golden Isles, had a famous slave named Bu Allah or Ben-Ali. Ben-Ali was Muslim, wrote in Arabic, and spoke the Foulah language. He and Tom are "intimate friends."

Hodgson brought his study to an end with a concise discussion of several of the lesser Berber dialects

Hodgson's contribution to knowledge was noteworthy, for he was the first American to address himself to a study of any of the numerous African peoples.[21] Be that as it may, a few comments need to be added to his work. First, later scholarship has shown that when the Phoenicians, Greeks, and Romans came to the North African coast, they found the Berbers already on the scene. With the coming of the Arabs in the seventh century, the Berbers scattered. Many of them became Arabized and embraced the religion of Islam. While many adopted the Arabic language, others retained their original tongue and preserved their ancient customs and traditions. George Peter Murdock lists twenty-nine peoples who have retained the Berber language. He remarked that the Berber culture was strongest in the mountain region inhabited by the Kabyles and others.[22]

Hodgson alluded to the possible future publication of his material on the Tuarycks, but it has proven impossible to determine if the French Geographic Society published his material on these tribal people. Filling in some of the interstices on the Tuarycks that Hodgson omitted, Murdock said of them that they retained the language of their Berber ancestors and some of the outstanding tribal customs. But in other respects they abandoned their past and developed a cultural matrix that was neither Berber nor Arab. He characterized them as "camel nomads" who organized "in migratory bands rather than settled villages" and lived in "tents." While their political organization represented a synthesis of Berber and Arab, their system of property and inheritance was unique. They also had a caste system that more readily fits the Arab custom than the Berber.[23]

Concerning Hodgson's relation with James Hamilton Couper, it is a pity that the manuscript collections of neither reflected their ties. Couper was one of the best known men in the South, and his library was considered one of the best private libraries in the country. Couper shared many of Hodgson's interests, being a geologist, archaeologist, and an avid reader of state history. In fact, he assisted William B. Stevens in his History of Georgia, a task that also interested Hodgson.[24] Couper's fame spread, and he knew Sir Charles Lyell, the noted English geologist who visited Hopeton. The Englishman described Couper's head driver, Old Tom, as a "man of superior intelligence." Tom provided a valuable service for his master during the War of 1812. When Admiral Cockburn of the Royal Navy offered Couper's slaves their freedom, Old Tom persuaded at least half of them to remain in the service of their master.[25]

No less talented than Tom was Thomas Spalding's Ben-Ali, whose command of Arabic was supplemented with his ability to speak both English and French. He, too, provided valuable assistance to his master during the War of 1812 when he led the island's slaves to help defend his master's plantation from the British. According to tradition his most valued possessions were his Koran and his prayer rug.[26] Inasmuch as many of his descendents are living today in coastal Georgia and retain a long folk tradition of their own, is it not possible that some enterprising black historian might put together a family history not unlike Alex Haley's well-received Roots?

Having established himself as an authority on several of the more interesting peoples of Sub-Saharan and Northern Africa, Hodgson was invited in 1845 to present to the New York Historical Society a paper entitled "Remarks on the Past History and Present Condition of Morocco, Algiers, and the Barbary Regencies." Addressing the society's membership on 1 October, Hodgson presented first a brief sketch of the history of the peoples of the Barbary coast from earliest times to the coming of the Ottoman Turks. He then discussed at some length the depredations of the Barbary corsairs of Morocco, Algiers, Tunis, and Tripoli, pointing out that American and European shippers engaged in the Mediterranean trade only after paying tribute to the pirates. But following the American War of 1812 with Great Britain, Commodore Stephen Decatur employed naval force and ended the payment of tribute and the enslaving of American seamen for all time. Hodgson asserted that the present condition of the Barbary states was one of weakness, with Tripoli and Tunis being under the Turks, Algiers a French colony, and Morocco a much subdued independent Arab state. Hodgson concluded his paper with an encomium of William Shaler, touching on his scholarly accomplishments and acknowledging his indebtedness to him for guiding his own early ventures into the realm of Middle Eastern scholarship and language study.[27]

Hodgson's work in the area of African studies gained for him a wide reputation. Writing in London in 1848, R. G. Latham published a Report on the Present State and Recent Progress of Ethnographical Philology, giving Hodgson due credit for his study on the Foulahs in his Notes on Northern Africa, the Sahara, and the Soudan. He observed that Hodgson had presented to M. D'Avezac a manuscript treating the manners, culture, customs, and language of the Tuarycks, together with an Arabo-Tuaryck vocabulary.[28]

Hodgson also enjoyed a good repute in France, for he represented the State of Georgia as a Commissioner to the Paris Exposition in 1855, for which he received a large engraved medal commemorating the event. On 15 November of that year the French government conferred on him La Medaille des Recompenses in recognition of his services rendered to French colonial officials in Algiers. (Apparently Hodgson had made available to these agents of French imperialism his wealth of material on the geography and culture of the Algerian people). The certificate of conferral was signed by Emperor Napoleon III.[29]

The autumn of 1854 found Hodgson back in New York City to present a paper to the Ethnological Society of New York. Addressing the body of members at a regular meeting on 13 October, Hodgson chose as his topic "The Gospels, Written in the Negro Patois of English, with Arabic Characters, by a Mandingo Slave in Georgia."[32] Hodgson related that he had gained possession of a manuscript written by a Negro slave named London, the property of a native of Savannah. This man was an educated Muslim who had been of the Mandingo tribe that inhabited the Western Sudan.[33]

Hodgson observed that this manuscript is the only attempt "ever made by an African Mohammedan to use the letters of the Koran, the first book of his religious instruction, in transcribing the Gospel, the book of his second instruction and conversion, and in the adopted dialect of his land of captivity." He then made some interesting observations about the nature of slaves in the Sudan, asserting that in that region three-fourths of all the inhabitants are slaves, with slavery being the law rather than the exception. He claimed that the region's inhabitants who lived between the tenth and twentieth parallels were Negroes who were of the Muslim faith and that they had been taught Arabic by their teachers. Below the twentieth parallel, the people were pagans. As a result of the predominance of the Muslim faith in parts of the Sudan, Hodgson noticed that a "feeble wave of Mohammedanism and Koranic letters once reached these shores from Africa, bearing with it some humble captives, and then sunk in the moving sands." He then cited several examples. Hodgson recorded that in the early part of the 18th century Prince Job, a Muslim Foulah, was liberated at Annapolis by the British government and returned to his own land. In 1835 Abd-er-rachman, better known as Prince Paul, was liberated by his master in the State of Mississippi, and returned to Liberia by the Colonization Society. Hodgson noted that he had in his possession an Arabic letter from this Foulah prince. Unfortunately, a search of Hodgson's papers did not disclose this letter. Hodgson also made note of the Foulah African known as Omar, or Moro, as he is more commonly known. He is described by Hodgson as "a good Arabic writer" who "reads the Bible in that language with some correctness and intelligence." Hodgson observed that he had received letters from Omar, but that the latter had refused to spend time with him in order that he might further investigate his use of language. The Foulah replied to Hodgson: "White mon catchee one time; not catchem two time." Hodgson also related a brief biographic sketch of Ben-Ali, the Foulah slave who was the property of Thomas Spalding of Sapelo.

He declared that he also possessed a Foulah among his battery of household servants, admitting that he neither read nor wrote. Hodgson appended to his essay the opening lines of the Gospel of John as translated from the Arab characters of London:

>    Fas chapta ob jon.
>
>    Inde beginnen wasde wad:
>
>    andde Wad waswid Gad,
>
>    ande wad was Gad.

Hodgson related an interesting point in his translation: "When this manuscript was first submitted to me, I naturally looked for Arabic words to be expressed by the letters. I could detect none; and I abandoned the interpretation. When, however, the characters and vowels had been carefully turned into Roman letters, I discovered by sound, what the eye had failed to perceive."[34]

In 1858 Hodgson again addressed the Ethnological Society of New York. Appearing before the membership in early November, Hodgson took as his subject Dr. Henry Barth's recent exploration of Central Africa, the results of which Barth presented to the world of scholarship in five volumes.[35] The sole survivor of a five-year exploration of Central Africa, Barth had mapped and described his 10,000 mile itinerary that included an exploratory venture from Lake Chad to the remote and mysterious city of Timbuktu. Following a discussion of his geographic notes, Hodgson launched into a discussion of Barth's ethnological findings. He noted that Barth had confirmed his own ethnographic discoveries concerning some of the Negro tribes of the Sudan, and of the Tuarycks and Toureg. While he questioned some of Barth's conclusions relative to the Tuarycks and the Berbers, he nevertheless praised him for supplying the scholarly community with a quantity of interesting data. Hodg-

son concluded his address with a lengthy discussion
of the etymology of numerous words in the Tuaryck
and Toureg, within the context of the new data that
Barth had amassed for scholars.[36]

There seems to have been no hiatus in Hodgson's
scholarly activities during the four-year period of
the Civil War, even though he would have been cut off
from his colleagues in New York and New England who
shared his scholarly pursuits. That the war did not
mark a complete dearth of scholarly activity on Hodgson's part is evidenced by his having branched out
into studies of Sanscrit and Hebrew. He delivered a
lecture, "The Science of Language: Sanscrit and Hebrew, the Two Written Primitive Languages Compared,"
which was published at Newport in 1868. As indicated
by the prefatory comment to the paper, Hodgson probably delivered it to the Georgia Historical Society
at sometime during the war, for he noted that "the
essay was written amidst the clang of arms." It contains a brief allusion to the Southern Confederacy.[37]
The essay tells us something about Hodgson's _weltanschauung_ and about his depth of knowledge concerning
the study of philology. First of all, he posited that
the "doctrine of race is involved in that of language; and this essay claims for the races speaking
the Aryan tongues, to which English belongs by inheritance, all political, ethnical and social supremacy."
Hodgson's feeling and acceptance of Anglo-Saxon superiority became increasingly popular among scholars of
the nineteenth century. Little wonder that Hodgson
accepted this attitude, for he was but a creature of
his time. Secondly, Hodgson's essay does exhibit a
rather profound understanding of the study of comparative philology, a science which he noted was
peculiar to the nineteenth century. He averred that
the study of vocabularies and grammars of the various languages "determines that there is a relationship between the different races of men who speak
those languages." Although addressing himself to
the relationship between Sanscrit and Hebrew, he

nevertheless used his background in African studies to make one important point. He wrote: "The language of each distinct race has its own grammatical laws from which it cannot escape. An African will use French or English words, but he will connect them in speech as nature taught him to connect the words of the African language." He declared that "An educated African may be taught to speak English grammatically; but never will a whole people, conquered or subject, acquire the syntax of the dominant race. Hence, in this process of adopting a foreign language, an irregular or inchoate form of speech is produced. Here, it is called patois; and on the shores of the Mediterranean, Lingua Franca. Language," Hodgson concluded, "is the expression of the intellectual development of a race." Carrying his discussion a point further, Hodgson observed that comparative philology has its peculiar laws. One is that a similarity of words indicates the relationship of languages. Another is that common grammar and vocabularies presume the identity of races. Hodgson asserted that language is broken down into families, and that the Indo-European or Arayan and Shemitic (Semitic) constitute two of the large families. The Sanscrit is placed in the former family, while Hebrew falls into the latter. The other families include the Turanian and the Allophylian. For the purpose of showing the kinship of various languages in a given family, Hodgson compared words in Sanscrit, Latin, and German to indicate the definite similarity. He asserted that the comparison might be enlarged to include English and Greek.

Moving on to a discussion of the Semitic language, Hodgson advised his hearers that it was "strikingly different" from the Indo-European languages, both in grammatical structure and in vocabularies. Since the dissimilarity was so great, Hodgson observed that under the first law of linguistics, there was no affinity between the two languages. Taking Hebrew as an example of the Semitic family, he declared that the language of the Jews was more stereotyped and inflexible. It expressed only two conditions of time--

Savannah    149

the past and the future.

Although Hodgson's lecture contained material that was common knowledge to the philologist and constituted little more than a "cursory and imperfect review," as he described it, nevertheless, it is worthy of note that Hodgson was a man whose knowledge of philology was gained by virtue of his own efforts, for he had received no training in a school of higher education. Too, the essay does indicate that he had a competent grasp of a new field of study that had its origins in Europe during the first half of the nineteenth century.

In addition to continuing his interest in philology Hodgson broadened the scope of his intellectual activity by associating with the small coterie of intellectuals in the coastal Georgia city of Savannah. The city of this period has been well described by J. Fred Waring, who pointed out that the ambitious mercantile element that made up the city's leadership had little time for scholarly pursuits during the early years of the nineteenth century. But by the 1830s and 1840s the city began to enjoy a fuller cultural life. Oddly enough, Waring did not include Hodgson's name in the list of notable Savannahians who made any pretence of scholarly or academic interests.[38] Perhaps this was an oversight on Waring's part, or perhaps it was due to the incomplete state of his manuscript at the time of his death.

In the 1840s Savannah was a city of some eleven thousand souls. While hardly an intellectual Mecca on a par with New York, Boston, Washington, or Charleston, nevertheless Waring tells us that the city could hardly be described as an intellectual desert.[39] Shortly before Hodgson's arrival in the city in 1842, a small group of men in 1839 formed the Georgia Historical Society. On 9 January 1843 Hodgson joined the Society, thus associating with such notable men as James M. Wayne, Justice of the United States Supreme Court, and John Macpherson Berrien, a former

Attorney General and later U.S. Senator from Georgia. Hodgson played an energetic role in the Society's activities, and in the year of his election he was delegated by the Society to attend a meeting of the National Institute at Washington, where he read a paper entitled "Memoir on the Megatherium and Other Extinct Gigantic Quadrupeds of the Coast of Georgia with Observations on Its Geologic Features."[40] This paper on fossil remains falls within the purview of the science of geology and indicates the scope of Hodgson's broad intellect. He admitted that he only became aware of the interesting fossil remains on the coast of Georgia following his arrival in Savannah. Contact with James Hamilton Couper of Hopeton Plantation and with Dr. J. C. Habersham of Savannah whetted his interest in this field of study. Hodgson's decision to publish this paper was prompted by a suggestion by Sir Charles Lyell, the eminent British geologist, who in 1846 visited Savannah and urged Hodgson to publish his findings.[41] A subsequent service for the Society was Hodgson's editing of Benjamin Hawkins' travel account, A Sketch of the Creek Country in 1798. This account was then published in the Society's Collections.[42] But perhaps Hodgson's greatest service to the Georgia Historical Society was the leading role that he played in securing a number of colonial records related to the founding of Georgia and to the colony's early years.[43] Ultimately, the acquisition of these records provided William Bacon Stevens with the raw material that he required to write his History of Georgia, which appeared in 1847, and the second volume which was published in 1859.

But although he continued a scholarly way of life, Hodgson did not close himself off from the affairs of the world in which he lived. He was living during a momentous period in this country's history, one that saw the fires of sectionalism build up and ultimately consume the nation in a four-year civil war. As the administrator of his wife's vast estate, Hodgson was compelled to take a keen interest in the slavery question, for his wife's property included plantations in Jefferson, Burke, and Jenkins counties, all of which were located in the fertile region of eastern Georgia. Hodgson's extensive correspondence with James H. Hammond, governor and later United States Senator from South Carolina, delineates the development of his thinking on the question of slavery and the overall topic of sectionalism. Although Hodgson could be classed as a moderate on the question of slavery, his correspondent in Washington was a staunch supporter of slavery. For example, in 1849 at the time the Wilmot Proviso, a recommendation to resolve the question of slavery in the territories was under discussion, Hodgson wrote that he opposed the Proviso, but would not dissolve the Union if it passed the Congress.[44] In the following year, when the Nashville Convention of Southern states met to discuss a regional response to the passage of the famous Compromise of 1850, Hodgson wrote to Hammond, elected to attend the Convention as a delegate, that he hoped it would never assemble, but in the event that it did that he (Hammond) would take a moderate course.[45] Yet Hodgson did wish to preserve the system of slavery, for he wrote Hammond that he supported Senator John C. Calhoun's law of equilibrium whereby the country would be governed by a dual presidency that would preserve the rights of the minority South and its peculiar institution.[46] Under this proposal each section would have a president, with each having veto power over proposed legislation. Even so, the enigmatic Hodgson wrote Hammond that he did favor the Compromise of 1850, because the American system of government was built on compromise and the nation must continue to pursue that course of action. "This Union," Hodgson declared, "will last longer than either of us, and in that sentiment I shall rest confident."[47] Writing later during the crucial decade in the aftermath of the repeal of the Missouri Compromise, the conciliatory Hodgson posited that the North was right to resent the repeal of the compromise which resulted from the issuance of the decision of Supreme Court Chief Jusice Roger B. Taney in the case of <u>Dred Scott v. Sanford</u>. He said that the nation needed a conciliatory man.[48] One wonders what reaction Senator Hammond had to Hodgson's moderate position. But he made his position clear, for in an address to the Senate on 4 March 1858 he declared that the South must retain the institution of slavery, for society must have a class "to perform the drudgery of life," one "requiring but a low order of intellect," one that "constitutes the very mud-sill of society." He held that the world depended on cotton. Hammond concluded in a peroration that "no power on earth dares make war upon it. Cotton is king."[49] To Hammond's speech, Hodgson replied somewhat belatedly that the address had "taken all hearts by storm." Optimistic about the future of the republic, Hodgson wrote that even though he could see "the lowering clouds" still he was confident the Union would be preserved. He declared that if the question were open, he would oppose the continuation of the slave trade.[50] But following the November election which saw Abraham Lincoln elected on a platform unalterably opposed to the expansion of slavery into the territories, Hodgson changed his tune. While still in favor of a compromise based on a dual executive, he nevertheless swung into line behind the Southern move to secede. He acknowledged that "with regard to Georgia, I am decidedly of the opinion that she should at once absolve herself from allegiance as preparatory to a more perfect union, supposing that to be still within the range of possibilities."[51] However, the day would come when Hodgson would rue his decision to support secession.

As he took an interest in the growing sectional crisis attached to the question of slavery, so he also took an interest in other areas of public affairs and kept the company of men in high public office. For example, in November, 1846, following Hammond's unsuccessful bid for a U.S. Senate seat from South Carolina, Hodgson wrote that he had discussed with Langdon Cheves, former congressman from South

Carolina, retired state judge, attorney, architect, and for a while president of the United States Bank, and a notable citizen of his state who had rejected appointments as Associate Justice of the U.S. Supreme Court and to the U.S. Senate, Hammond's political future.[52] In the same letter, Hodgson mentioned that he had entertained Richard Pakenham, British Minister in Washington, at a dinner party.[53] It seems that Pakenham had come to Georgia along with Anthony Barclay, British Consul in New York, owner of a Georgia plantation, and friend of Hodgson, and that Hodgson had entertained the two British officials and their wives at the Telfair mansion in Savannah. Pakenham, it should be noted, had participated in the negotiations between the United States and Great Britain that led to the settlement of the Oregon question in June of that year. Concerning the settlement of the Oregon question, there is an interesting footnote to this matter in which Hodgson might have played a small role. It seems that Hodgson had received a letter from a George Sumner of Boston, then in Paris, related to the sentiments of the conciliatory Lord Aberdeen, British Foreign Minister, concerning the Oregon question. Sumner wrote that in January 1846 Lord Aberdeen told a friend who communicated to him that he (Aberdeen) was desirous of arranging the Oregon question by May by accepting the 49th parallel as a compromise line. Hodgson related the above to Secretary of State James Buchanan in May 1846, admitting that while the matter might be of little concern, he was aware that frequently "statesmen disclose to private confidence, sentiments which they cannot, from their position, throw before the public."[54] Inasmuch as Hodgson's letter reached Buchanan before the June settlement and concurrently with Pakenham's disclosure to Buchanan of the conciliatory nature of Lord Aberdeen, it might be that Hodgson's disclosure carried some positive weight with the Secretary of State. This is pure speculation.

Hodgson also maintained contact with his old patron,

Judge McLean, writing that he applauded General Zacary Taylor's exploits in the War with Mexico and indicating Whiggish sentiments.[55] McLean was not Hodgson's only contact in Washington, for in 1847 Daniel Webster, former Secretary of State who furthered Hodgson's career by sending him to Tunis, wrote Hodgson that he was coming to Savannah and appreciated the opportunity to visit him. He wrote: "It will give me great pleasure to see you and your family." Webster urged that Hodgson go to no great trouble on his behalf since he wanted to make a quiet, private visit "to see the country and see the people."[56] A subsequent letter indicated that Webster, then serving in the U.S. Senate, appreciated Hodgson's willingness to come to Augusta to accompany him on his journey to the coastal city.[57] The newspapers make only small mention of Webster's Savannah visit. But Hodgson thought so well of his former chief that he traveled from New York to Washington at the time of the Senator's death in 1852 "to pay reverence to him."[58]

Hodgson also maintained an interest in diplomatic appointments in the State Department. Writing to Senator Hammond in 1858, Hodgson lamented that John Porter Brown, his old competitor at Constantinople, had "an outrageous accumulation of offices." Apparently jealous of Brown's accomplishments, Hodgson was referring to Brown's serving as Secretary of Legation, dragoman, and Consul General at Constantinople. (Hodgson had little cause for jealousy, for ultimately Brown died penniless in Constantinople, and his wife was given a small sum of money by a friend to return to the United States). Hodgson also retained hopes of a diplomatic appointment, for he advised Hammond that if he were appointed to a ministerial post or as chief of a diplomatic mission that he (Hodgson) would like to go along as secretary-interpreter.[59]

In addition to his scholarly interests and his concern with public affairs, Hodgson had further responsibility in managing his wife's vast estate. Alexander Lawrence has described the Telfair family as the richest in Savannah.[60] The family's wealth was based on bank, shipping, railroad, and industrial stocks, real estate in Savannah, plus three plantations in Burke, Jefferson, and Jenkins counties. These latter holdings caused Lawrence to characterize the Telfair family as the city's largest slave holder.[61] For this reason Hodgson was compelled to make many inspection trips to the plantations and to take an interest in cotton prices and in the planting of crops that would build up his soil. He was, indeed, a progressive planter. Although having a considerable number of slaves to look after, Hodgson also represented extensive business interests on behalf of the Telfair family. An examination of Savannah newspapers and of the Hodgson-Hammond correspondence indicates that Hodgson was a member of the board of directors of the Bank of the State of Georgia, of the Albany and Gulf Railroad, of the Augusta and Waynesboro Railroad, of the Savannah-Florida Trunkline Railroad, and of the Savannah-to-Augusta Railroad. In addition he oversaw the family's extensive real estate holdings in the city. He also administered a large block of stock in a steamship line that ran from Savannah to New York.[62] Although directing the family plantations and thus representing the slaveholding class of the Ante-Bellum South, Hodgson seems to have believed that slave labor was uneconomical and that the future of the South lay in industry. Because of his business associations and of his views on the commercial future of the South, Hodgson, along with John Macpherson Berrien, James P. Screven, Robert Habersham, Alexander R. Lawton, and Francis S. Bartow, attended the Southern Commercial Convention in Charleston in March 1854 as representatives from Savannah. The delegates urged their respective state legislatures to pass state laws in favor of manufacturing, shipping, railroads, and education.[63]

Although he represented the business orientation that would characterize the men trying to establish a "New South" based on industry and commerce in the post-Civil War era, Hodgson also represented the slave-holding class. While a moderate, he nevertheless supported secession when it came, and the Civil War, with its accompanying destruction and deprivation, wrought havoc with the fortunes of the Telfair family and its head. To chronicle the last days of the war in Savannah, Hodgson left behind a small diary entitled "Memoranda of the War."[64] This is an excellent account of the depths to which the South had sunk during the closing days of the war.

The army of General William Tecumseh Sherman took Atlanta in the summer of 1864 and then set out on its famed or ill-famed "March to the Sea." As the troops approached Savannah, Hodgson began to experience the real problems that accompany war. On 24 November he attempted to visit his plantation near Millen, for his overseer had written that Sherman's approach compelled him to join the Confederate army. Hodgson's attempted visit was a failure, for the approaching Union army cut him off and he was forced to return to Savannah. He reported that Sherman's troops had burned one of the Telfair family plantations near Louisville.[65] As the Northern army came closer to Savannah, Anthony Barclay, the British consular official and friend of Hodgson whose Rockingham plantation was burned by the Union troops, moved into the Telfair mansion on St. James Square in Savannah. He promptly raised the British flag over the residence.[66] This was done with a view to keep Confederate troops from raiding the house, for the city was in a state of chaos. Hodgson reported that Confederate troops were loitering about the city and that the city streets were full of Negro slaves who had come into the city from the surrounding countryside. Because he had heard a rumor that some Confederates, bent on illicit gain, would try to break into the Telfair house with a view to looting it, Hodgson and his family were compelled to arm themselves and to stand guard throughout the night of 21 December.[67]

Federal troops entered the city of Savannah, and

Savannah 157

General Sherman promptly presented it to President
Abraham Lincoln as a Christmas present. Though it was
an untidy, somewhat bedraggled city, nevertheless it
was a most welcome gift. For the taking of Savannah
constituted the end of the long campaign that had
begun in the early days of the war when Union strate-
gists had sought to break into Tennessee, take the
railroad centers at Chattanooga and Atlanta, and then
sweep through Georgia, thus destroying the South's
granary and cutting off the coastal South from the
states on the Gulf of Mexico.

Shortly after Sherman arrived in the city, Hodgson
paid a visit on the 27th of December to the General.
Hodgson hoped to obtain a pass from the General to
visit the family plantations and then return to the
city following the tour of inspection. The General
said that the exigencies of war prevented him from
complying with his wish. Otherwise, Hodgson found
General Sherman to be "perceptive" and "genial" and
a man whose character was marked by "innate benevol-
ence." The General said that in cases of extreme
need, the army would issue rations to those whites
and blacks until such time as regular business would
restore the market economy.[68]

Although the Telfairs were the richest family in
the city, Hodgson recorded that they were in need.
He wrote: "With our pockets charged with Confederate
money, we have not a sixpence with which to buy the
most ordinary articles."[69] Destitution prevailed in
the city, and Hodgson left behind a rather graphic
account of the sad plight of the people. "Many physical privations" are present. "Men's minds turned
inward upon themselves. Many have lost all in the
war." He lamented the loss of wealth and property
and bemoaned the fact that this loss would result in
the absence of the leisure time so necessary to
maintaining a fervent intellectual life. "Science
and letters would suffer," Hodgson concluded.[70] To
make matters worse, the city experienced a disastrous fire when the Confederate arsenal went up in

flames. Hodgson reported that departing Confederates had sent guerrillas into town to blow up the storehouse of ammunition to deny it to the approaching Union army. He noted that some 1,000 shells and a quantity of fixed ammunition had been left behind. At 12:30 a.m. on the morning of 28 January the fire started and consumed some one hundred dwellings and came close to destroying the Telfair mansion.[71] Hodgson recorded that matters grew worse, for with the departure of Sherman's army for South Carolina, the people of Savannah began to realize the onerous burden of living in an occupied city. Depression was to be found on every hand among the citizenry, which had to live day-by-day with the blue-clad troops of the Union army.[72]

Although Hodgson and his family most assuredly suffered economically due to the turn of events that accompanied the closing days of the Civil War, their life style suffered relatively little as compared to the vast majority of the people. While Hodgson did not seem to maintain the same degree of interest in scholarship in the postwar era as he did in the pre-Civil War days, he did continue to administer the family's somewhat diminished holdings in bonds and other securities in the aftermath of the war.

Hodgson's way of life was apparently not so radically altered that he could not indulge in his annual yearning to travel to the North, for it was in New York City that he died on 26 June 1871, while on his annual "northern tour." His health had not been good in recent months prior to his journey. His body was returned to Savannah on 30 June, and the Reverend I. S. K. Axson of the Independent Presbyterian Church of Savannah presided over the funeral in the Telfair mansion on 1 July. Pallbearers included General Alexander Lawton, General Henry R. Jackson, William P. Hunter, and John Screven. He was interred in the Telfair family vault in the Bonaventure Cemetery.[73]

# 9
# SUMMARY

Chapter 9

Summary

What can be said of William Brown Hodgson's life? Without formal, higher education, Hodgson obtained a sufficient grasp of foreign languages and of the budding science of philology to attain a position in the nation's consular service. He used this position during the vital period of out-reach that followed the War of 1812 and ventured abroad to secure the information about the Middle East that his country so badly needed to maintain its position in the community of nations trading with that remote region. He gathered a wealth of knowledge about Oriental languages, customs, manners, geography, and diplomatic practice. His knowledge of Oriental languages and his subsequent writings in this area, plus his writings on the language and peoples of Africa placed him in the elite echelon of men whose interest far transcended the natural boundaries of the United States.

That Hodgson was able to maintain himself in the country's consular service during a period when there was little structure and rationale behind appointments, tenure, and advancement, is a testimony of his astute grasp of the realities of politics. He knew full well that victory went, not to those who had a secure grasp of knowledge in their respective fields,

but to those who had sufficient connections in high
political places to secure for themselves place and
position in the absence of a system. One must marvel at his ability to secure positions under both
Democratic and Whig administrations. While it is
true that Hodgson did on occasion make claims about
his expertise that he could not substantiate, it
would appear that the lack of a well-structured consular service that included the basic rudiments of a
system caused him to overstep the bounds of wisdom.
Indeed, lacking such a system, the life of a consular
officer in the nineteenth century was a precarious
existence.

Hodgson is to be further congratulated for making
a wise marriage into a wealthy family that guaranteed him the leisure and resources so necessary to
the continued pursuit of scholarship. That he was
able to balance a life of scholarship with a life
of service to the community, and at the same time administer his wife's vast economic holdings, is a credit to him. Indeed, a notice in a local newspaper
commented that on moving to Savannah Hodgson became
an "ardent advocate of the development of the resources of the city." Further, that he "identified
with all her great interests."[1] In the closing years
of his life, he is reputed to have been "a quiet retiring gentleman of the old school, with rather stately manners. He was very studious in his habits, but
also took an active interest in public affairs."[2]

As a tribute to Hodgson's scholarly life and his
contributions to the community in which he lived out
his last years, Margaret Telfair Hodgson, his widow,
built Hodgson Hall, which houses the archives and
library of the Georgia Historical Society, in his
memory. Today the west wall of that edifice is adorned with a life-size portrait of Hodgson, done
posthumously. It is fitting that the artist shows
him standing in a library, with his hand extended to
an Arabic manuscript.

# NOTES

NOTES

Preface

1. James A. Field, Jr., America and the Mediterranean World, 1776-1882 (Princeton, 1969), pp. 442-443.
2. David H. Finnie, Pioneers East: The Early American Experience in the Middle East (Cambridge, 1967); Joseph L. Grabill, Protestant Diplomacy and the Near East: Missionary Influence on American Policy (Minneapolis, 1971); Robert L. Daniel, American Philanthropy in the Near East, 1820-1960 (Athens, Ohio, 1970); L. C. Wright, United States Policy Toward Egypt, 1830-1914 (New York, 1969); A. L. Tibawi, American Interests in Syria, 1800-1901: A Study of Educational, Literary and Religious Work (New York, 1966); and Roy F. Nichols, Advance Agents of American Destiny (Philadelphia, 1956).
3. Nichols, Advance Agents, p. 12.
4. John A. DeNovo, "Researching American Relations with the Middle East: The State of the Art, 1970," 243-264, in Milton O. Gustafson, ed., The National Archives and Foreign Relations Research (Athens, Ohio, 1974).
5. Warren Frederick Ilchman, Professional Diplomacy in the United States (Chicago, 1961), pp. 1-3; William Barnes and John Heath Morgan, The Foreign Service of the United States: Origins, Development, and Functions (Washington, 1961), pp. 51, 55, 57, and 68; Robert D. Schulzinger, The Making of the Diplomatic Mind: The Training, Outlook, and Style of United States Foreign Service Officers (Middletown, Conn., 1975), p. 1.
6. Ephraim Speiser, The United States and the Near East (Cambridge, 1952), pp. 248-249; Luella J. Hall, The United States and Morocco, 1776-1957 (Metuchen,

N. J., 1971), pp. 90, 136, and 240. However, L. C. Wright maintains that the U.S. was not guilty of this practice in Egypt. He quotes a dispatch from Hodgson verifying this fact. Wright, United States Policy Toward Egypt, p. 53.

7. Lawrence E. Gelfand, "A Merit System for the American Diplomatic Service, 1896-1930," a paper presented at the annual conference of the Organization of American Historians, St. Louis, Mo., April 1976.

Chapter 1. Introduction

1. Nichols, Advance Agents, pp. 11-12.
2. Ilchman, Professional Diplomacy, pp. 1-2.
3. Schulzinger, The Making of the Diplomatic Mind, p. 1.
4. Barnes and Morgan, The Foreign Service of the United States, pp. 52, 27, 68, 89; Ilchman, Professional Diplomacy, pp. 3, 16, 17, 26-28, 35; and Schulzinger, The Making of the Diplomatic Mind, pp. 1-5.
5. Barnes and Morgan, The Foreign Service of the United States, p. 5 and Schulzinger, The Making of the Diplomatic Mind, pp. 70-71.
6. Hall, The United States and Morocco, pp. 90, 136, 240 and Wright, United States Policy Toward Egypt, pp. 52-55.
7. Ilchman, Professional Diplomacy, p. 4 and Barnes and Morgan, The Foreign Service of the United States, p. 53.
8. Barnes and Morgan, The Foreign Service of the United States, pp. 81-82.
9. Samuel Flagg Bemis, John Quincy Adams and the Foundations of American Foreign Policy (New York, 1949), I, 256-257.
10. Ibid., I, 255-257, 264.

Notes     167

11. Application File of William Brown Hodgson, Record Group, 59, National Archives. Also see F. S. Key-Smith, <u>Francis Scott Key: Author of the Star Spangled Banner</u> (Washington, 1911), p. 24.

12. On Carnahan, see <u>Dictionary of American Biography</u>, III. 498 and J. P. Jackson, <u>The Chronicles of Georgetown</u> (Washington, 1878), pp. 143-144.

13. <u>Select Dialogues of Lucian with Notes in Latin and Greek</u> (Philadelphia, 1806) in Hodgson papers, Telfair Family Papers, Hodgson Hall, Savannah, Ga.

14. See clipping in ibid., #523, Box 29.

15. For brief sketches of Hodgson's life, see <u>Dictionary of American Biography</u>, First Supp., pp. 412-413 and Leonard L. Mackall, "William Brown Hodgson," <u>Georgia Historical Quarterly</u>, XV (Dec. 1931), 324-345.

16. Hodgson to Adams, 29 Apr. 1824 and Cook to Adams, 28 Apr. 1824, Application File of W. B. Hodgson.

17. Hodgson to Peter S. Duponceau, 20 June 1829, Peter S. Duponceau papers, Historical Society of Pennsylvania, Philadelphia, Pa.

18. The papers of John McLean, Library of Congress, contain numerous letters pointing to Hodgson's dependence on McLean's patronage.


Chapter 2.  Apprenticeship at Algiers


1. <u>We the People</u>, 9 Aug. 1828, 2:4.

2. Nichols, <u>Advance Agents</u>, Chapters 6 and 7 and "Diplomacy in Barbary," <u>Pennsylvania Magazine of History and Biography</u>, LXXIV (Jan. 1950), 113-141.

3. Clay to Shaler, 29 Dec. 1825, James F. Hopkins, ed., <u>The Papers of Henry Clay</u> (Lexington, Ky., 1972), IV, 952.

4. Clay to Hodgson, 14 Jan. 1827, Department of State Instructions to Barbary States. Hereafter cited

as DSI.
5. Clay to Shaler, 18 Feb. 1826, ibid.
6. John Quincy Adams, Memoirs of John Quincy Adams, edited by Charles Francis Adams (New York, 1969 reprint edition), VII, 106-107.
7. Hodgson to Daniel Brent, 11 Feb. 1826, Department of State Dispatches, Algiers. Hereafter cited as DSD.
8. Hodgson to Peter Force, 23 Feb. 1826, Peter Force papers, Library of Congress.
9. Hodgson to Force, 25 June 1826, ibid.
10. Hodgson to Clay, 12 Apr. 1826, DSD.
11. Nichols, Advance Agents, p. 111
12. Hodgson to Force, 25 June 1826, Force papers and Hodgson to John McLean, 28 June 1826, John McLean papers, Library of Congress. McLean, Hodgson's patron and benefactor, had the letter published in the National Intelligencer as having been written by a "young American gentleman in Algiers." National Intelligencer, 7 Oct. 1826, 3:4.
13. Nichols, Advance Agents, pp. 111-112.
14. Hodgson to Force, 25 June 1826, Force papers.
15. Hodgson to Force, 23 and 25 June 1826, ibid.
16. Shaler to Clay, 1 June 1826, DSD.
17. Journal of U.S. Consulate, Algiers, 1 June 1826. Hereafter cited as Journal. Hodgson to Clay, 1 June 1826, DSD.
18. Charles F. Gallagher, The United States and North Africa: Morocco, Algeria, and Tunis (Cambridge, Mass., 1963), pp. 59-63.
19. Journal, 22 April 1826.
20. Ibid., 7 Jan. 1826, 18 May 1826, 25 June 1826.
21. Ibid., 21 Sep. 1826 and Hodgson to Force, 25 June 1826, Force papers.
22. Nichols, Advance Agents, pp. 135-136.
23. Shaler to Duponceau, ___ July 1826, William Shaler papers, Historical Society of Pennsylvania, Philadelphia, Pa.
24. Hodgson to Clay, 1 June 1826, DSD.
25. Shaler to Clay, 1 June 1826, ibid.
26. Hodgson to Clay, 1 Dec. 1826 ibid.
27. Hodgson to Brent, 4 Oct. 1826, ibid.

28. Shaler to Hodgson, 29 Jan. 1827, Shaler papers; Hodgson to Clay, 2 May 1827, 24 Aug. 1827, DSD.
29. Hodgson to Clay, 2 May 1827; on Hodgson's propensity for acquiring languages, Leonard Mackall wrote that he (Hodgson) mastered thirteen languages and spoke nine fluently. Mackall, "William Brown Hodgson," 326.
30. Hodgson to Clay, 14 May 1827, DSD.
31. Hodgson to Clay, 5 Oct. 1827, ibid.
32. Shaler to Hodgson, 25 Mar. 1828, ibid.
33. Shaler to Clay, 8 May 1828, ibid.
34. Hodgson to Clay, 10 Apr. 1828, ibid; Hodgson to Shaler, 27 Sep. 1828, Shaler papers.
35. Hodgson to Clay, 10 April 1828, DSD.
36. Nichols, Advance Agents, pp. 135-137.
37. Shaler to Duponceau, 15 Feb. 1828, 10 June 1828, Duponceau papers.
38. These letters are in the Duponceau papers and four of them were published in Transactions of the American Philosophical Society, IV, (New Series), 1834, 1-48. Notice of the publication of these letters appeared in the African Repository, VII (June 1831), 109-113. Several of the letters appeared in the North American Review (July 1832), 54-74.
39. See "Note on William B. Hodgson" by Dr. Cyrus Adler, Journal of American Oriental Society, 15 Apr. 1892, ccx-ccxi; F. W. Newman, "Notes on Libyan Languages," Journal of the Royal Asiatic Society, (1880) 417-427; Robert N. Cust, A Sketch of the Modern Languages of Africa (London, 1883), pp. 101-102; John Pickering, Presidential Address at First Annual Meeting of American Oriental Society in 1843, Journal of American Oriental Society, I, 18-19 and Franklin Edgerton, Proceedings of American Philosophical Society, 87 (1943), 31.
40. The original of the letter from Hodgson to Duponceau, 18 May 1828, is in the Duponceau papers, but was published in Transactions of the American Philosophical Society, IV (1834), 1-14.
41. Shaler to Duponceau, 12 Dec. 1828, Duponceau papers.
42. Hodgson to Duponceau, 28 May 1828, ibid.

43. Hodgson to Duponceau, 1 Sep. 1828, ibid., and was published in Transactions of the American Philosophical Society, IV, (New Series), 1834, 14-21.
44. Shaler to Duponceau, 2 Dec. 1828, Duponceau papers.
45. Hodgson to Duponceau, 20 Jan. 1829, ibid., and was published in Transactions of the American Philosophical Society, IV, (New Series), 1834, 22-26.
46. Hodgson to Duponceau, 1 June 1829. This letter was reprinted in the African Repository, V (Jan. 1830), 337-341. Hodgson continued his interest in the Foulahs with the publication of The Foulahs of Central Africa and the Slave Trade (Savannah, 1843).
47. Hodgson to Duponceau, 1 April 1829, Duponceau papers. This letter was published in Transactions of the American Philosophical Society IV, (New Series) 1834, 26-48.
48. Hodgson sold the Book of Genesis and the Four Gospels, as translated into Berber, to the British and Foreign Bible Society in 1831 for one hundred and fifty pounds. Leonard Mackall reckons this to be a modest sum, given the fact that Hodgson and his Taleb Sidi Hamet worked on the project for two years. In 1833 the Bible Society printed 250 copies of twelve chapters of St. Luke. Mackall, "William Brown Hodgson," 327, 342.
49. Hodgson to Duponceau, 4 Sep. 1829, Duponceau papers.
50. Hodgson to Duponceau, 1 Apr. 1829, 18 Oct. 1829, ibid.
51. Duponceau to Shaler, 21 Sep. 1829, Arthur Bining papers, Historical Society of Pennsylvania. See also Shaler to Duponceau, 2 May 1829, Duponceau papers. Hodgson's paper, "Grammatical Sketch and Specimens of the Berber Lanuage: Preceded by Four Letters on Berber Etymologies," was read to the members of the American Philosophical Society on 2 Oct. 1829.
52. Duponceau to Lee, 31 July 1829, DSD.
53. Hodgson to Duponceau, 4 Sep. 1829, Duponceau papers.
54. Hodgson to Duponceau, 4 Sep. 1829, ibid.

55. Hodgson to Adams, 29 Jun. 1829 and Hodgson to Duponceau, 22 Sep. 1829, ibid.
56. A Catalogue of Arabic, Turkish, and Persian Manuscripts: Private Collection of Wm. B. Hodgson (Washington: Duff Green, 1830). This rare pamphlet is in the American Oriental Society Library, Sterling Memorial Library, Yale University. It was presented by William Shaler to John Pickering, founder of the AOS. The collection described in the catalogue was sold by Hodgson to the British Museum in 1833-1834. See Mackall, "William Brown Hodgson," 339. I have in my collection of materials related to Hodgson a lengthy description of this collection furnished me by the British Museum.
57. Shaler to Hodgson, 20 Mar. 1828, copy in the Shaler papers.
58. Barnes and Morgan, Foreign Service of the United States, pp. 77-79.
59. Gallagher, The United States and North Africa, p. 63; Nichols, Advance Agents, p. 140; and William Spencer, Algiers in the Age of the Corsairs (Norman, Okla., 1976), p. 149.
60. Hodgson to Clay, 24 June 1827, DSD.
61. Hodgson to Clay, 5 Oct. 1827, ibid.
62. Hodgson to Clay, 10 Apr. 1828, ibid.
63. Hodgson to Clay, 10 Apr. 1828, ibid.
64. Journal, 7 Feb. 1827.
65. Ibid., 15 April 1827.
66. Hodgson to McLean, 28 Feb. 1827, 20 Apr. 1828, McLean papers.
67. Hodgson to McLean, 10 July 1827, ibid.
68. Hodgson to McLean, 12 April 1828, ibid.
69. Hodgson to McLean, 29 June 1829, ibid.
70. Hodgson to Adams, 29 June 1829 in Duponceau papers.
71. Shaler to Clay, 8 May 1828, DSD.
72. Shaler to Duponceau, 12 Dec. 1828, Duponceau papers.
73. Shaler to Van Buren, 20 May 1829, DSD.
74. Shaler to Duponceau, 5 May 1829, Duponceau papers; Duponceau to Shaler, 18 May 1829, Shaler papers; Shaler to Duponceau, 25 May 1829, Duponceau papers.

75. Hodgson to Duponceau, 4 Sep. 1829, 22 Sep. 1829, ibid.
76. Martin Van Buren, Autobiography of Martin Van Buren, ed. by John D. Fitzpatrick (2 vols. New York, 1973 reprint edition), I, 231-232.
77. Hodgson to Van Buren, 1 May 1829, DSD.
78. Hodgson to Van Buren, 4 July 1829, ibid.
79. Ilchman, Professional Diplomacy, pp. 26-28.
80. James D. Richardson, ed., A Compilation of the Messages and Papers of the Presidents, 1789-1908 (11 vols., Washington, 1908), II, 449.
81. On Major Lee, see Dictionary of American Biography, XI, 109. On Hodgson, see Hodgson to Duponceau, 20 June 1829, 22 Sep. 1829, Duponceau papers.
82. John Spencer Bassett, The Life of Andrew Jackson (New York, 1931), p. 411.
83. Hodgson to Van Buren, 4 July 1829, DSD.
84. Van Buren to Hodgson, 24 July 1829, Department of State Consular Instructions.
85. Hodgson to Van Buren, 17 Nov. 1829, DSD.
86. Hodgson to Shaler, 9 Jan. 1830, Shaler papers.

Chaper 3.  A Tour at the State Department

1. Hodgson to Shaler, 12 Jan. 1830, Shaler papers.
2. Hodgson to Shaler, 14 Jan. 1830, ibid.
3. Bassett, The Life of Andrew Jackson, p. 412 and Marquis James, Andrew Jackson: Portrait of a President (New York, 1937), p. 198.
4. James, Andrew Jackson, p. 216.
5. Adams, Memoirs, VIII, 170-171. I have not been able to determine that Hodgson studied Hebrew while in Algiers. But he most assuredly had a knowledge of Hebrew as indicated by the debate with Henry Watterson that is mentioned in chapter one of this study.
6. Hodgson to Shaler, 20 Feb. 1830, Shaler papers.
7. On the city of Washington, see James, Andrew Jackson, p. 327 and Claude G. Bowers, The Party

Battles of the Jackson Period (Boston, 1922), pp. 2-29.
8. James, Andrew Jackson, pp. 266-267.
9. Published in Washington in 1830.
10. Mackall, "William Brown Hodgson," 339.
11. Ibid., 344 and National Intelligencer, 8 Jan. 1830.
12. Letter from Peter S. Duponceau and John Vaughn to American Philosophical Society, 15 Jan. 1830, American Philosophical Society Archives.
13. Hodgson to APS, 16 April 1830, ibid.
14. Adams, Memoirs, VIII, 227. Actually, Hodgson had supervised the translation of four of the Gospels.
15. Mackall, "William Brown Hodgson," 342.
16. Hodgson to Gurley, 28 Feb. 1830, American Colonization Society Records, Series 1, Vol. 21
17. Bassett, The Life of Andrew Jackson, p. 194.
18. Thomas A. Bailey, A Diplomatic History of the American People (New York, 1958), p. 194 and Hunter Miller, ed., Treaties and Other International Acts of the United States of America (Washington, 1933), III, 507-521, 541-598. Also see Lester Langley, "Jacksonian America and the Ottoman Empire," Muslim World, LXVIII (Jan. 1978), 45-56.
19. Van Buren, Autobiography, I, 270.
20. Charles Oscar Paullin, Diplomatic Negotiations of American Naval Officers, 1778-1883 (Baltimore, 1912), pp. 123-124; James A. Field, Jr., America and the Mediterranean World, 1776-1882 (Princeton, 1969), p. 113; Leland James Gordon, American Relations with Turkey, 1830-1930 (Philadelphia, 1932), p. 8; and L. C. Wright, United States Policy Toward Egypt, 1830-1914 (New York, 1969), p. 27.
21. Finnie, Pioneers East, p.26; Gordon, American Relations with Turkey, pp. 8, 9; and Wright, United States Policy Toward Egypt, p. 27.
22. Paullin, Diplomatic Negotiations, pp. 123-124; Finnie, Pioneers East, pp. 30-33.
23. Field, America and the Mediterranean World, p. 138.

24. Ibid., p. 146.
25. Gordon, *American Relations with Turkey*, p. 10; Paullin, *Diplomatic Negotiations*, pp. 144-148; and Miller, ed., *Treaties*, III, 541-598.
26  Paullin, *Diplomatic Negotiations*, p. 150.
27. Finnie, *Pioneers East*, p. 63.
28. Ibid., p. 65 and James A. Hamilton, *Reminiscences* (New York, 1869), pp. 207-216.


Chapter 4.  Service in Constantinople


1. Van Buren to Hodgson, 15 April 1831, Department of State Instructions, Turkey.
2. Jackson to Sultan Mahmud of Turkey, 15 Apr. 1831, Andrew Jackson papers, Library of Congress; Van Buren to Reis Effendi, 15 April 1831, Martin Van Buren papers, Library of Congress; Van Buren to Reis Effendi, 15 April 1831, ibid.
3. Hodgson to McLean, 21 April 1831, McLean papers.
4. Hodgson to Van Buren, 25 April 1831, 4 May 1831, Department of State Dispatches, Turkey. Hereafter cited as DSD.
5. John Israel and Henry N. Lundt, *Journal of a Cruise in the U.S.S. Delaware, 74, in the Mediterranean* (Port Mahon, Minorca, 1835), pp. 75-80.
6. See *Dictionary of American Biography*, Vol. 15, 83-85; David Dixon Porter, *Memoir of Commodore David Porter of the United States Navy* (Albany, N.Y., 1875); Archibald D. Turnbull, *Commodore David Porter* (New York, 1929); and David F. Long, *Nothing too Daring: A Biography of Commodore David Porter, 1780-1843* (Annapolis, 1970).
7. Hodgson to Livingston  30 June 1831, DSD
8. Porter to Livingston, 13 June 1831, ibid.
9. Finnie, *Pioneers East*, pp. 82-83.
10. Porter to Livingston, 11 July 1831, DSD.

11. Turnbull, Commodore David Porter, p. 308 and Porter, Memoir of Commodore David Porter, p. 399.
12. James E. DeKay, Sketches of Turkey in 1831 and 1832 (New York, 1833), p. 298 and Porter to Livingston, 17 Aug. 1831, DSD.
13. Finnie, Pioneers East, p. 85; E. D. G. Prime, Memoirs of Rev. William Goodell, Late Missionary of the A. B. C. F. M. at Constantinople (New York, 1876), pp. 114, 122; DeKay, Sketches of Turkey, p. 175; David Porter, Constantinople and Its Environs (New York, 1835), I, 86; and Porter to Livingston, 17 Aug. 1831, DSD.
14. Porter, Constantinople and Its Environs, I, 20-21 and Finnie, Pioneers East, p. 85.
15. Porter, Constantinople and Its Environs, I, 21-24.
16. Porter to Livingston, 11 Aug. 1831, DSD.
17. Paullin, Diplomatic Negotiations, pp. 150-151.
18. Porter to Livingston, 11 Aug. 1831, DSD.
19. Stanley Lane-Poole, The Life of Lord Stratford de Redcliffe (London, 1890), I, 509.
20. Hodgson to Livingston, 12 Sep. 1831, DSD.
21. Porter to Livingston, 26 Sep. 1831, ibid; Porter, Constantinople and Its Environs, I, 153-154. For an interesting comment on the role of the dragoman, see DeKay, Sketches of Turkey, pp. 282-286.
22. Miller, ed., Treaties, III, 588-592.
23. DeKay, Sketches of Turkey, pp. 299-300.
24. Hodgson to Livingston, 12 Sep. 1831, DSD and Porter to Livingston, 23 Sep. 1831 and 26 Dec. 1831, ibid.
25. Porter, Constantinople and Its Environs, I, 43-49.
26. Porter, Memoir of Commodore David Porter, pp. 402-403 and Turnbull, Commodore David Porter, p. 308.
27. Porter, Constantinople and Its Environs, I, 49-53.
28. See Finnie, Pioneers East, pp. 84-85 and Paullin, Diplomatic Negotiations, pp. 151-152.
29. Porter to Livingston, 5 Oct. 1831, DSD.
30. Hodgson to Van Buren, 26 Jan. 1831, Application File of W. B. Hodgson, Records of the Department of State.

31. Hodgson to Livingston, 21 Jun. 1831, ibid.
32. Hodgson to Livingston, 24 Sep. 1831, ibid.
33. Stevenson to Van Buren, 6 Jan. 1831, ibid.
34. Duponceau to Van Buren, 9 Jan. 1831 and to Livingston, 27 Jan. 1832, ibid.
35. Carnahan to Van Buren, 10 Jan. 1831, ibid.
36. Hodgson to Porter, 16 Oct. 1831, DSD.
37. Hodgson to Livingston, 19 Jan. 1832, ibid.
38. Livingston to Porter, 25 Mar. 1832, DSI.
39. Navoni to Livingston, 10 Mar. 1832, DSD.
40. Hodgson to Livingston, 29 Feb. 1832, ibid.
41. Hodgson to Livingston, 24 Mar. 1832, ibid.
42. Hodgson to Livingston, 5 Apr 1832, 21 Jun. 1832, ibid.
43. Cary Corwin Conn, "John Porter Brown, Father of Turkish-American Relations, An Ohioan at the Sublime Porte, 1832-1872," Ph.D. dissertation, Ohio State University, 1972, pp. 12, 13.
44. Hodgson to Livingston, 21 June 1832, DSD.
45. Porter to Hodgson, 7 July 1832, ibid.
46. Hodgson to Porter, 11 July 1832, 13 July 1832, 20 July 1832, Papers of the American Legation at Constantinople. Hereafter cited as Post Papers.
47. Hodgson to Porter, 11 Aug. 1832, ibid.
48. Hodgson to Porter, 16 Aug. 1832, ibid.
49. Porter to Livingston, 18 Aug. 1832, DSD.
50. Conn, "John Porter Brown," pp. 13-14.
51. Long, A Biography of Commodore David Porter, p. 307.
52. Porter to Livingston, 11 Nov. 1832, quoted in Conn, "John Porter Brown," p. 18.
53. Finnie, Pioneers East, p. 87; Long, A Biography of Commodore David Porter, p. 312; and DeKay, Sketches of Turkey, p. 285.
54. Long, A Biography of Commodore David Porter, p. 311.
55. Elizabeth Cabot Kirkland, "Letters" in Proceedings of the Massachusetts Historical Society, 2nd ser, (Boston), XIX (1906), 440-504.
56. Porter, Constantinople and Its Environs, II, 29; Conn, "John Porter Brown," pp. 12, 13.
57. Hodgson to Livingston, 1 Dec. 1832, DSD.

58. Hodgson to Livingston, 7 Dec. 1832, ibid.
59. Porter to Livingston, 27 Oct. 1832, ibid.
60. Porter to Hodgson, 6 Dec. 1832, ibid.
61. Turnbull, Commodore David Porter, p. 310. On the misnumbering of dispatches, see Hodgson to Porter, 11 May 1833, DSD.
62. Hodgson to Livingston, 25 June 1833, ibid.
63. Long, A Biography of Commodore David Porter, pp. 313-314.
64. Porter to Hodgson, 4 Mar. 1833, DSD.
65. Sydney Nettleton Fisher, The Middle East: A History (New York, 1969), pp. 274-275.
66. Hodgson to Porter, 11 Mar. 1833, DSD.
67. Porter to Hodgson, 11 Mar. 1833, ibid.
68. Hodgson to Porter, 11 Mar. 1833, ibid.
69. Porter to Hodgson, 13 Mar. 1833, ibid.
70. Hodgson to Porter, 18 Mar. 1833, ibid.
71. Porter to Hodgson, 18 Mar. 1833, ibid.
72. Hodgson to Porter, 18 Mar. 1833, ibid.
73. Porter to Hodgson, 8 April 1833, ibid.
74. Hodgson to Livingston, 9 May 1833, ibid.
75. Hodgson to Livingston, 9 May 1833, ibid.
76. Cohen to Porter, undated, ibid.
77. Porter to Cohen, 27 May 1833, 30 May 1833, ibid.
78. Cohen to Porter, 31 May 1833, ibid.
79. Hodgson to Livingston, 8 June 1833, ibid.
80. Porter to Hodgson, 11 May 1833, ibid.
81. Hodgson to Livingston, 11 May 1833, ibid.
82. Hodgson to Livingston, 24 May 1833, ibid.
83. Hodgson to Livingston, 19, 21 June 1833, ibid.
84. Barnes and Morgan, The Foreign Service of the United States, p. 76.
85. Porter to Hodgson, 20 June 1833 and Porter to Livingston, 24 June 1833, DSD.
86. Porter to Livingston, 28 June 1833, ibid.
87. Porter to Livingston, 9 July 1833, ibid.
88. Hodgson to Porter, 8 July 1833, ibid.
89. Porter to Hodgson, 9 July 1833, ibid.
90. Hodgson to Porter, 9 July 1833, ibid.
91. Porter to Livingston, 27 Mar. 1833, ibid.
92. Porter to Livingston, 19 June 1833, ibid.

93. Porter to Livingston, 11 July 1833, ibid.
94. Porter to Hodgson, 11 July 1833, ibid.
95. Hodgson to McLane, 12 July 1833, ibid.
96. Porter to Hodgson, 3 Aug. 1833, ibid.
97. Hodgson to McLane, 10 Sep. 1833, ibid.
98. Van Buren to Porter, 15 Apr. 1831, DSI. See also Miller, ed., Treaties, III, 588-592 for a discussion of Hodgson's ability as a translator.
99. Hodgson to Livingston, 25 June 1833, DSD.
100. Long, A Biography of Commodore David Porter, pp. 311-314.
101. Miller, ed., Treaties, III, 590.
102. Cited and quoted in ibid., 592.
103. Ibid., 592.
104. Barnes and Morgan, The Foreign Service of the United States, pp. 82-85.
105. Hodgson to Livingston, 8 May 1833, DSD. Dispatches from Hodgson to Livingston, dated 22 Mar. 1832 and 18 Aug. 1832, DSD, indicate that Porter was active in providing arms to the Turks. A letter from Porter to President Jackson, 7 Oct. 1831, further substantiated Hodgson's suggestion that Porter was trafficking in arms with the Turks. Porter to Jackson, 7 Oct. 1831, David Porter papers, Library of Congress.
106. Hodgson to Livingston, 9 June 1833, DSD.
107. Hodgson to Livingston, 25 June 1833, ibid.
108. Porter to McLane, 9 Aug. 1833, ibid.
109. McLane to Porter, 10 Oct. 1833, DSI.
110. Porter to Hodgson, 28 Oct. 1833, DSD.
111. Hodgson to Patterson, 30 Oct. 1833, 3 Nov. 1833, ibid.
112. Porter to Patterson, 1 Nov. 1833 and Patterson to Porter, 6 Nov. 1833, ibid.
113. See Hodgson's statement dated 9 Nov. 1833, Porter's statement dated 18 Nov. 1833 and Patterson to Porter, 18 Nov. 1833, ibid.
114. Hodgson to Patterson, 19 Nov. 1833 and Patterson to Hodgson, 19 Nov. 1833, ibid.
115. Hodgson to McLane, 18 Nov. 1833, 10 Dec. 1833, and 7 Jan. 1834, ibid.
116. Forsyth to Porter, 10 Sep. 1835, DSI.

117. McLane to Porter, 31 Mar. 1834 and Forsyth to Porter, 2 May 1835, *ibid*.
118. Barnes and Morgan, The Foreign Service of the United States, p. 94.


Chapter 5. A Mission to Egypt


1. On the conflict between the Sultan and Muhammad Ali, see Fisher, The Middle East, pp. 272, 274-276, 282-283. On the movement of the American Mediterranean squadron to the east, see Field, America and the Mediterranean World, pp. 192-193.
2. Patterson to Livingston, 19 June 1833, DSD.
3. McLane to Hodgson, 10 Oct. 1833, Department of State, Special Missions, I. On Hodgson's mission to Egypt, see Field, America and the Mediterranean World, pp. 193-194; Wright, United States Policy Toward Egypt, pp. 35-37; Finnie, Pioneers East, pp. 92-93; and Merritt Henry Wriston, Executive Agents in American Foreign Relations (Baltimore, 1929), pp.556-557 and 707-708; and Thomas A. Bryson, "William Brown Hodgson's Mission to Egypt, 1834," West Georgia College, Studies in the Social Sciences, XI (June 1972), pp. 10-17.
4. McLane to Porter, 10 Oct. 1833, DSI.
5. Hodgson to McLane, 4 June 1834, DSD.
6. Hodgson to McLane, 10 June 1834, *ibid*.
7. Hodgson to McLean, 9 June 1834, McLean papers.
8. Hodgson to McLane, 7 July 1834, DSD.
9. Hodgson to Porter, 6 June 1834, Post Papers; Porter to Mrs. Porter, 20 Mar. 1835, Porter papers.
10. Forsyth to Porter, 2 May 1835, DSI.
11. Hodgson to McLane, 25 Aug. 1834, DSD.
12. Hodgson to McLane, 28 Sep. 1834, *ibid*.
13. Finnie, Pioneers East, pp. 92-93.
14. Hodgson to Forsyth, 2 Dec. 1834, DSD.
15. Hodgson to Forsyth, 2 Dec. 1834, *ibid*.
16. Hodgson to Forsyth, 13 Dec. 1834, *ibid*.

17. Hodgson to Forsyth, ibid.
18. Hodgson to Forsyth, 2 Mar. 1835, ibid.
19. Wright, United States Policy Toward Egypt, pp. 37-39.
20. Field, America and the Mediterranean World, p. 381.
21. Copies of the Sketch are in Hodgson's papers, Georgia Historical Society and in the DeRenne Collection at the University of Georgia Library.

## Chapter 6. A Washington Interlude, with Missions to Tangier, Peru, and Germany

1. Hodgson to Forsyth, 24 Dec. 1836, Application File of W. B. Hodgson.
2. Forsyth to Hodgson, 8 Aug. 1835, Department of State Instructions, Barbary States.
3. See Hall, The United States and Morocco, p. 160 and Miller, ed., Treaties, IV, 65.
4. "Journal, 11 Aug-Nov 1835--Travel from Washington to Tangier," Hodgson papers. Hereafter cited as Journal.
5. Ibid., 19 Aug. 1835.
6. Leib to Forsyth, 19 Sep. 1835, Department of State Dispatches, Tangier. Hereafter cited as DSD.
7. Hall, The United States and Morocco, pp. 160-62.
8. Hodgson to Forsyth, 23 Sep. 1835, DSD.
9. Journal, 14 Oct. 1835.
10. Leib to Forsyth, 14 Oct. 1835, DSD.
11. Journal, 8, 9, 12, 14 Oct. 1835.
12. Ibid., undated.
13. Journal, 24 Oct. 1835 and Leib to Forsyth, 10 Dec. 1835, DSD.
14. Hodgson to Forsyth, 29 Nov. 1835, ibid.
15. Leib to Forsyth, 10 Dec. 1835, ibid.
16. Ibid.
17. Hall, The United States and Morocco, pp. 160-62.
18. Hodgson to Forsyth, 29 Nov. 1835, DSD.

19. Hodgson to Forsyth, 24 Dec. 1836, Application File of W. B. Hodgson.
20. Hodgson to Forsyth, 9 Jan. 1837, ibid.
21. Hodgson to Jackson, 1 Mar. 1837, ibid.
22. Letter of recommendation from R. E. Parker to Forsyth, 26 June 1837, ibid.
23. Letter from Hodgson to (addressee not listed), 10 May 1836, American Philosophical Society Archives.
24. Hodgson to Duponceau, 10 Apr. 1835, ibid.
25. Hodgson to John Vaughn, 21 Sep. 1837, ibid. Also see Terry Alford, Prince Among Slaves (New York, 1977), pp. 170 and 276. Alford says that the translation was properly made by Hodgson, whom he characterizes as "the first American Sudanist." Alford suggests that the African actually translated the opening sura of the Koran.
26. See Dictionary of American Biography, First Supp., I, p. 412. See also Journal of Royal Asiatic Society, IV, 115-129.
27. Forsyth to Hodgson, 12 Oct. 1837, Department of State Instructions, Peru and Forsyth to Thornton, 14 Oct. 1837, ibid.
28. See Hodgson's "Journal: 1837, Travel from Washington to Peru," Hodgson papers. Hereafter cited as Journal.
29. Journal, 18 Jan. 1838.
30. Bartlett to Hodgson, 2 April 1838, Department of State Dispatches, Peru.
31. Hodgson to Forsyth, 2 Apr. 1838, DSD.
32. Bartlett to Forsyth, 5 April 1838, ibid. Hodgson had taken possession of the treaty and dispatches which had been placed in the hands of Captain McKeever of the Falmouth.
33. Bartlett to Captain McKeever, 5 April 1838; McKeever to Bartlett, 5 April 1838, ibid.
34. Journal, 25-30 April, 1, 2 May 1838. Hodgson suffered from an illness which he described in his Journal as "soroche," a respiratory ailment that frequently struck the newcomer to the extreme heights of the Andes Mountains.
35. Bartlett to Forsyth, 5 July 1838, DSD.
36. Court Martial Proceedings begun on 8 Sep. 1842

in the Case of W. B. Hodgson's Complaint versus Captain Henry Ballard, U. S. Navy. A copy of this document is in the Hodgson papers.

37. Journal, 9 Aug. 1838.
38. Ibid., undated.
39. Ibid., 24 Aug. 1838 and Miller, ed., Treaties, IV, 102.
40. Hodgson to Forsyth, 23 April 1839, Application File of W. B. Hodgson.
41. Forsyth to Hodgson, 8 Aug. 1840 and Forsyth to Wheaton, 8 Aug. 1840, Department of State Instructions, German States. See also Miller, ed., Treaties, IV, 251, 271.
42. Hodgson to Forsyth, 10 Aug. 1840, Application File of W. B. Hodgson.
43. Wheaton to Forsyth, 15 Oct. 1840, Department of State Dispatches, German States.
44. Hodgson to Stevenson, 1 Nov. 1840, Andrew Stevenson papers, Library of Congress.
45. McLean to Harrison, 10 Mar. 1841, Application File of W. B. Hodgson.
46. Hodgson to McLean, 7 April 1841, McLean papers.

Chapter 7. American Consul at Tunis

1. Hodgson to McLean, 13 Sep. 1841, McLean papers. There is a short paragraph in Cary Conn's dissertation, saying that Hodgson desired to regain his old position at Constantinople. But Conn arrives at the conclusion that Hodgson used his influence to have Heap posted to Constantinople in order that he (Hodgson) might obtain the post at Tunis. In view of Hodgson's letters to Judge McLean, it would appear that Conn accepts a conspiratorial conclusion about Hodgson's motivations. See Conn, "John Porter Brown," pp. 35-36.
2. Webster to Hodgson, 22 Sep. 1841, Department of State Instructions to Barbary States.

3. The National Institution to which Hodgson refers, was founded in 1840, and it was instrumental in the founding of the Smithsonian Institution in 1846 at which time it turned over its collections to the Smithsonian. See Lilla Mills Hawes and Albert S. Britt, Jr., editors, The Search for Georgia's Colonial Records (Savannah: Georgia Historical Society, 1976), p. 124.
4. Hodgson to McLean, 27 Sep. 1841, McLean papers.
5. Hodgson to McLean, 31 Oct. 1841, ibid.
6. Hodgson to Webster, 1 Nov. 1841, Department of State Dispatches, Tunis. Hereafter cited as DSD.
7. Gallagher, The United States and North Africa, pp. 69-71.
8. Consular Journal, Tunis, 11-14 Feb. 1842, DSD.
9. Hodgson to Webster, 15 Feb. 1842, ibid.
10. Hodgson to Webster, 16 Feb. 1842, ibid.
11. Hodgson to Webster, 1 Mar. 1842, ibid.
12. Hodgson to Webster, 1 Mar. 1842; Hodgson-Heap Memorandum, 20 Feb. 1842; and Hodgson to W. W. Andrews, 14 Apr. 1842, ibid.
13. Hodgson to Webster, 14 Apr. 1842, ibid.
14. Hodgson to Webster, 28 April 1842, ibid.
15. Journal of "Travel to Naples, Florence, etc." entry for 28 May 1842.
16. Ibid., 30 May 1842.
17. Ibid., 29 May 1842.
18. See Dictionary of American Biography, XVIII, 361-362.
19. Hodgson to Tyler, 3 July 1842, a rough draft of which is in the Hodgson papers; Hodgson to Webster, 3 July 1842, DSD.
20. Savannah Daily Georgian, 5 Aug. 1842, 3:1

Chapter 8.  Savannah and
            Scholarly Activities

1. See Dictionary of American Biography, 1st Supp.,

p. 412.
2. Mackall, "William Brown Hodgson," p. 329.
3. See James Cowles Prichard, Researches into the Physical History of Mankind (London, 1837), II, Note 16.
4. H. Corabeuff to Hodgson, 20 Oct. 1836, Hodgson papers.
5. Hodgson to D'Avezac, 10 Nov. 1838, quoted in Mackall, "William Brown Hodgson," p. 332.
6. Gordon Wright, France in Modern Times: 1760 to the Present (Chicago, 1967), pp. 147-148.
7. Letter dated 30 May 1974 from Professor Terry Alford of Northern Virginia Community College to the author. Alford has recently published Prince Among Slaves, a biography of Abd al-Rahman Ibrahima, a Fula slave from present-day Guinea. This is perhaps the first book-length biography of an African in American slavery to appear. This work was published by Harcourt, Brace, Jovanovich in 1977.
8. August Meier and Elliott Rudwick, From Plantation to Ghetto (New York, 1976), pp. 7-35.
9. Ibid., pp. 36-39.
10. Letters from Terry Alford to the author, dated 6 Oct. 1976 and 28 August 1977.
11. For an interesting contemporary description of the Fulani, see George Peter Murdock, Africa: Its Peoples and Their Culture History (New York, 1959), pp. 413-421.
12. W. B. Hodgson, "The Foulahs of Central Africa and the Slave Trade," (Savannah, 1843). A copy of this essay is in the DeRenne Collection, University of Georgia Library.
13. Murdock, Africa: Its Peoples and Their Culture History, p. 414.
14. Ibid., p. 415.
15. Dictionary of American Biography, XIV, 564-65.
16. Hodgson to W. W. Greenough, 30 Sep. 1843, American Oriental Society papers, Yale University Library, New Haven, Conn.
17. Hodgson to Greenough, 3 May 1844, ibid.
18. Hodgson to E. P. Salisbury, 16 July 1846, ibid.

19. William B. Hodgson, Notes on Northern Africa, the Sahara, and Sudan (New York: Wiley and Putnam, 1844).

20. I have not been able to find a copy of this letter in the Hodgson papers.

21. Letter dated 28 Aug. 1977 from Terry Alford to the author.

22. Murdock, Africa: Its Peoples and Their Culture History, pp. 111-115.

23. Ibid., pp. 405-409.

24. Burnette Vanstory, Georgia's Land of the Golden Isles (Athens, 1956), pp. 90-95.

25. Betsy Fancher, The Lost Legacy of Georgia's Golden Isles (New York, 1971), p. 152. Also see Caroline Couper Lovell, The Golden Isles of Georgia (Boston, 1939), Chapter VII.

26. Vanstory, Georgia's Land of the Golden Isles, p. 48.

27. William B. Hodgson, "Remarks on the Past History and Present Condition of Morocco, Algiers, and the Barbary Regencies," Proceedings of the New York Historical Society (1844), pp. 162-168.

28. R. G. Latham, Report on the Present State and Recent Progress of Ethnographical Philology (London, 1848). From the Report of the British Association for the Advancement of Science for 1847.

29. See Mackall, "William Brown Hodgson," p. 325. The Medal conferred upon William Brown Hodgson as Commissioner of the State of Georgia to the Paris Universal Exposition, 1855 and the Certificate, dated 15 Nov. 1855, for La Medaille des Recompenses conferred upon W. B. Hodgson and signed by Napoleon III are in the Hodgson papers.

30. Mackall, "William Brown Hodgson," p. 328.

31. Hodgson to Whitney, 12 April 1858, American Oriental Society papers.

32. William Brown Hodgson, "The Gospels, Written in the Negro Patois of English, with Arabic Characters, by a Mandingo Slave in Georgia," (1857). In DeRenne Collection, University of Georgia Library.

33. It is worthy of note that Kunta Kinte, the

hero of Alex Haley's Roots was also of the Mandingo tribe.

34. Hodgson, "The Gospels, Written in the Negro Patois of English," p. 10.

35. Dr. Heinrich Barth, to use his German first name, was one of the great explorers of Africa. Early in 1840 he set out on an English-sponsored expedition with James Richardson. Following the latter's death, Barth assumed charge of the expedition which had set out from Tripoli, crossed the Sahara, and explored the region between Lake Chad and the city of Timbucktu. In spite of ill health, Barth traveled some 10,000 miles, recording his experiences in the five volume work Travels and Discoveries in North and Central Africa (1857-1858) which contain a vast amount of anthropological, historical, and linguistic information, as well as geographical data. See Encyclopedia Britannica, Vol. I, 1842.

37. Hodgson, "The Science of Language," iv.

38. J. Fred Waring, Cerveau's Savannah (Savannah, 1973), pp. 68-76.

39. Waring, Cerveau's Savannah, p. 69.

40. Published in New York by Bartlett and Welford in 1846. I located a copy of this work in the DeRenne Collection, University of Georgia Library.

41. See preface to the aforementioned paper on the Megatherium, located in the DeRenne Collection.

42. Mackall, "William Brown Hodgson," p. 326.

43. See Lilla Mills Hawes and Albert S. Britt, Jr., editors, The Search for Georgia's Colonial Records (Savannah, 1976), pp. 15, 22, 37, 48, 64, 66, 84, 121, 129, 132, 133, 134-135, 138, 140-141, 154, 166, 169, 173-174, 179, 203-204, 241. There are also several letters from Buckingham Smith, American Minister to Madrid, and from historian Jared Sparks to Hodgson concerning these Georgia records. Hodgson also solicited the advice and assistance of James A. Hammond, U.S. Senator from South Carolina, in the acquisition of Georgia's colonial records. See James A. Hammond papers, Library of Congress.

44. Hodgson to Hammond, 7 Oct. 1849, Hammond papers.

45. Hodgson to Hammond, 20 Mar. 1850, ibid.

46. Hodgson to Hammond, ibid.
47. Hodgson to Hammond, 6 Aug. 1850, ibid.
48. Hodgson to Hammond, 10 Nov. 1858, ibid.
49. On Hammond's career, see Dictionary of American Biography, VIII, 207-208. The speech is in Congressional Globe, 35 Cong, 1 Sess, p. 961
50. Hodgson to Hammond, 10 Nov. 1858, 20 Dec. 1858, Hammond papers.
51. Hodgson to Hammond, 6 Dec. 1860, ibid.
52. Hodgson to Hammond, 20 Nov. 1846, ibid.
53. Hodgson to Hammond, 20 Nov. 1846, ibid.
54. Hodgson to Buchanan, 12 May 1846, James Buchanan papers, Historical Society of Pennsylvania.
55. Hodgson to McLean, 20 Oct. 1846, McLean papers.
56. Webster to Hodgson, 5 April 1847, Daniel Webster Papers; Library of Congress has copies of these letters.
57. Webster to Hodgson, 10 May 1847, ibid.
58. Hodgson to Hammond, 20 Mar. 1850, Hammond papers.
59. Hodgson to Hammond, 2 Feb. and 12 Feb. 1858, ibid.
60. Alexander A. Lawrence, A Present for Mr. Lincoln: The Story of Savannah from Secession to Sherman (Macon, 1961), p. 220.
61. Ibid., p. 234.
62. Daily Morning News, 9 May 1860, 1:1; 8 Jan. 1861, 2:2; 3 Oct. 1863, 2:2; and 13 Feb. 1851, 2:4; Savannah Morning News, 16 Mar. 1869, 3:1; Savannah Daily Herald, 16 Feb. 1866, 2:2; and Hodgson to Hammond, 7 Oct. 1849, 12 Feb. 1858, Hammond papers.
63. Daily Morning News, 29 Mar. 1854, 2:2; 15 Apr. 1854, 1:1
64. William Brown Hodgson, "Memoranda of the War," in the Charles Colcock Jones papers, University of Georgia Library.
65. Ibid., entry dated 24 Nov. 1864.
66. Ibid., entry for 16 Dec. 1864.
67. Ibid., entry for 21 Dec. 1864.
68. Ibid., entry for 28 Dec. 1864.
69. Ibid., entry for 28 Dec. 1864.
70. Ibid., entry for 24 Jan. 1865.

71. Ibid., entry for 28 Jan. 1865.
72. Ibid., entry for 24 Jan. 1865.
73. Savannah Morning News, 27 June 1871, 1 July 1871, and 3 July 1871.


Chapter 9. Summary


1. Savannah Morning News, 27 June 1871.
2. Mackall, "William Brown Hodgson," p. 325.

# BIBLIOGRAPHY AND NOTE ON SOURCES

NOTE ON SOURCES

The manuscript collection of William Brown Hodgson is contained in the Telfair family papers at the Georgia Historical Society in Savannah. Inasmuch as Hodgson's niche in history is in large measure due to his activities on behalf of the Department of State in the Middle East, this biography is primarily concerned with those activities. Unfortunately, his papers do not reflect much light on this period of his life. Beyond a few scattered letters, an occasional account book, and a journal, the papers are almost totally devoid of useful references to his diplomatic career. This is all the more disappointing, for Hodgson associated with presidents, secretaries of state, congressmen, senators, justices of the Supreme Court, not to mention the wide range of dignitaries whom he met in Algiers, Turkey, Egypt, Tunis, and Tangier. As is so often the case, it has been necessary to consult other manuscript collections to find the documents necessary to support an account of Hodgson's diplomatic career. I have relied heavily upon the records of the Department of State. This rich and valuable collection is available on microfilm at the National Archives in Washington. The Diplomatic and Consular Instructions and Dispatches, the Application File of the subject, and the Instructions for Special Missions all provided a veritable collective, biographic sketch of Hodgson's career in the consular service of the United States.

In the course of his diplomatic activities, Hodgson engaged extensively in the study of Oriental languages and earned for himself considerable fame as an early American student of Arabic, Turkish, Persian,

and the esoteric Berber language. The archive of
the American Philosophical Society provided some insight into the extent of his activities. Of considerable aid in this area of his life were the collections of Peter S. Duponceau and William Shaler,
both housed in the Historical Society of Pennsylvania, Philadelphia. The papers of the American Oriental Society at Yale University also provided some
insight into Hodgson's work. John McLean, Supreme
Court justice, was Hodgson's benefactor throughout his
career in the consular service. His papers are located in the Library of Congress and provided a vital
account of Hodgson's use of McLean's high position to
maintain his position in the consular service.

Inasmuch as Oriental scholarship was so much a
part of Hodgson's life during and after his career
in the consular service, one would expect that his
papers would contain a complete collection of his
scholarly writings, but this is not the case. I
have relied on the Library of Congress, the Rhode
Island Historical Society, and on the DeRenne Collection at the University of Georgia for a complete
collection of his writings. The American Oriental
Society contains some of his writings and a list of
the oriental books and manuscripts that he presented
to the British Museum, as well as some of his manuscripts and books related to his studies.

Following Hodgson's resignation from the consular service, he resided in Savannah, and his manuscript collection contains a reasonable amount of
correspondence and other documents on which to base
a biography. However, a consultation of several
guides to manuscript collections indicates that Hodgson had a wide correspondence with important persons,
and his collection of papers does not reflect this in-
terchange. The papers of James H. Hammond, Library of Congress, were most useful in providing an
account of Hodgson's thoughts on national political
questions such as the vexing problem of sectionalism.
But as an example of the fragmentary nature of Hodg-

son's papers, there are no letters from Hammond in them.

Two works of considerable value in piecing together Hodgson's diplomatic career were David H. Finnie's Pioneers East: The Early American Experience in the Middle East (1967) and James A. Field's America and the Mediterranean World, 1776-1882 (1969). Finnie's elegantly written book provides a series of interesting vignettes of many early American travelers to the Middle East. One of these was of William B. Hodgson. Field's study, a classic in the field of American-Middle Eastern relations, supplies background material to the early American experience in the Middle East and also gives some detail about Hodgson's ventures there. Both works contain excellent bibliographies and frequent references to applicable State Department documents.

Finally, mention must be made of Treaties and Other International Acts of the United States of America, a work edited by David Hunter Miller. This valuable collection of American treaties, with the accompanying notes and commentary, supplies the historian with much-needed information relative to his work. I have found this multi-volume source to be rich in material related to Hodgson's activities in the Middle East, Latin America, and Europe.

BIBLIOGRAPHY

Primary Sources:

U.S. Government Manuscripts:

Records of the Department of State, Diplomatic Instructions, Turkey, I (1823-1859), National Archives, microfilm.

Records of the Department of State, Dispatches,

Turkey, (1818-1850), National Archives, microfilm.

Records of the Department of State, Instructions, Special Missions, National Archives, microfilm.

Records of the Department of State, Consular Dispatches, Algiers, (1785-1906), National Archives, microfilm.

Records of the Department of State, Consular Dispatches, Barbary, (1839-1906), National Archives, microfilm.

Records of the Department of State, Application File, National Archives, microfilm.

Records of the Department of State, Dispatches from United States Consuls in Tunis, (1797-1906), National Archives, microfilm.

Records of the Department of State, Dispatches from United States Consuls in Tangier, (1797-1906), National Archives, microfilm.

Records of the Department of State, Instructions to Barbary States, National Archives, microfilm.

Papers of the American Legation at Constantinople.

Records of the Department of State, Instructions to Peru, National Archives, microfilm.

Records of the Department of State, Dispatches from United States Consuls in Peru, National Archives, microfilm.

Records of the Department of State, Instructions to the German States, National Archives, microfilm.

Records of the Department of State, Dispatches from the German States, National Archives, microfilm.

Private Collections:

American Colonization Society Records, Library of Congress.

American Oriental Society Archives, Yale University, New Haven, Conn.

American Philosophical Society Archives, Philadelphia, Pa.

Arthur Bining papers, Historical Society of Pennsylvania, Philadelphia, Pa.

James Buchanan papers, Historical Society of Pennsylvania, Philadelphia, Pa.

Peter S. Duponceau Papers, Historical Society of Pennsylvania, Philadelphia, Pa.

Peter Force papers, Library of Congress.

James H. Hammond papers, Library of Congress.

John McLean papers, Library of Congress.

William Brown Hodgson papers, Georgia Historical Society, Savannah, Ga.

Andrew Jackson papers, Library of Congress.

Charles Colcock Jones Collection, University of Georgia Library.

David Porter papers, Library of Congress.

Keith Reid papers, University of Georgia Library.

William Shaler papers, Historical Society of Pennsylvania. Philadelphia, Pa.

Andrew Stevenson papers, Library of Congress.

Martin Van Buren papers, Library of Congress.

Daniel Webster papers, Library of Congress.

Published U.S. Documents:

Miller, Hunter, ed., Treaties and Other International Acts of the United States of America. 8 vols. Washington: Government Printing Office, 1933.

Richardson, James E., ed., A Compilation of the Messages and Papers of the Presidents, 1789-1908. 11 vols. Washington: Government Printing Office, 1908.

Miscellaneous:

Adams, John Quincy, Memoirs of John Quincy Adams: Comprising Portions of His Diary from 1795 to 1845. Edited by Charles Francis Adams. New York: Books for Libraries Press (1969 reprint edition).

Hopkins, James F., ed., The Papers of Henry Clay. 5 vols. Lexington: University of Kentucky Press, 1972.

Memoirs, Autobiographies and Diaries:

Hamilton, James A. Reminiscences. New York: Charles Scribners Co., 1869.

Israel, John and Lundt, Henry N. Journal of a Cruise in the U.S.S. Delaware, 74 in the Mediterranean. Port Mahon, Minorca, 1835.

Kirkland, Elizabeth Cabot. "Letters," in Proceedings of the Massachusetts Historical Society, 2nd Series, XIX (1906), 440-504.

Van Buren, Martin. Autobiography of Martin Van Buren, edited by John C. Fitzpatrick. 2 vols. New York: De Capo Press, 1973 reprint edition.

Biographies and General Works:

Alford, Terry. Prince Among Slaves. New York: Harcourt Brace Jovanovich, 1977.

Bailey, Thomas A. A Diplomatic History of the American People. New York: Appleton Century Crofts, 1971.

Barnes, William and Morgan, John Heath. The Foreign Service of the United States: Origins, Development, and Functions. Washington: Historical Office, Department of State, 1961.

Bassett, John Spencer. The Life of Andrew Jackson. New York: Macmillan Co., 1931.

Bemis, Samuel Flagg. John Quincy Adams and the Foundations of American Foreign Policy. 2 vols. New York: Alfred A. Knopf, 1956.

Bowers, Claude G. The Party Battles of the Jackson Period. Boston: Houghton Mifflin Co., 1922.

Bryson, Thomas A. American Diplomatic Relations with the Middle East, 1784-1975: A Survey. Metuchen, N.J.: Scarecrow Press, 1977.

Conn, Cary Corwin. "John Porter Brown, Father of Turkish-American Relations, An Ohioan at the Sublime Porte, 1832-1874," Ph.D. dissertation, Ohio State University, 1973.

DeKay, James E. Sketches of Turkey in 1831 and 1832, by an American. New York: Harper, 1833.

Fancher, Betsy. The Lost Legacy of Georgia's Golden Isles. New York: Doubleday, 1971.

Field, James A., Jr. America and the Mediterranean World, 1776-1882. Princeton: Princeton University Press, 1969.

Finnie, David H. Pioneers East: The Early American Experience in the Middle East. Cambridge: Harvard University Press, 1967.

Fisher, Sydney Nettleton. The Middle East: A History. New York: Alfred A. Knopf, 1969.

Gallagher, Charles F. The United States and North Africa: Morocco, Algeria, and Tunisia. Cambridge: Harvard University Press, 1963.

Gordon, Leland James. American Relations with Turkey, 1830-1930: An Economic Interpretation. Philadelphia: University of Pennsylvania Press, 1932.

Hall, Luella J. The United States and Morocco, 1776-1956. Metuchen, N.J.: Scarecrow Press, 1971.

Hawes, Lilla Mills and Britt, Albert S., Jr., eds. The Search for Georgia's Colonial Records. Savannah: Georgia Historical Society, 1976.

Jackson, R. P. The Chronicles of Georgetown. Washington: Private printing, 1878.

James, Marquis. Andrew Jackson: Portrait of a President. New York: Bobbs-Merrill, 1937.

Key-Smith, F. S. Francis Scott Key: Author of

the Star Spangled Banner. Washington: Key-Smith and Co., 1911.

Lane-Poole, Stanley. The Life of Lord Stratford de Redcliffe. London: Longmans, Green and Co., 1890.

Lawrence, Alexander A. A Present for Mr. Lincoln: Story of Savannah from Secession to Sherman. Macon: Ardivan Press, 1961.

Long, David F. Nothing Too Daring: A Biography of Commodore David Porter, 1780-1843. Annapolis: U.S. Naval Institute, 1970.

Meier, August and Rudwick, Elliott. From Plantation to Ghetto New York: Hill and Wang, 1976.

Murdock, George Peter. Africa: Its Peoples and Their Culture History. New York: McGraw-Hill, 1959.

Nichols, Roy F. Advance Agents of American Destiny. Philadelphia: University of Pennsylvania Press, 1956.

Paullin, Charles Oscar. Diplomatic Negotiations of American Naval Officers, 1778-1883. Gloucester, Mass.: Peter Smith, 1967 reprint edition.

Porter, David Dixon. Memoir of Commodore David Porter of the United States Navy. Albany, N.Y.: Munsell, 1875.

Prime, E. D. G. Memoirs of Rev. William Goodell: Late Missionary of the ABCFM at Constantinople. New York: Carter, 1876.

Schulzinger, Robert D. The Making of the Diplomatic Mind: The Training, Outlook and Style of United States Foreign Service Officers. Middletown, Conn.: Wesleyan University Press, 1975.

Speiser E. A. The United States and the Near East. Cambridge: Harvard University Press, 1952.

Spencer, William. Algiers in the Age of the Corsairs. Norman, Okla.: University of Oklahoma Press, 1976.

Turnbull, Archibald D. Commodore David Porter. New York: Century Co., 1929.

Vanstory, Burnette. Georgia's Land of the Golden Isles. Athens, Ga.: University of Georgia Press, 1956.

Waring, Joseph Frederick. Cerveau's Savannah. Savannah: Georgia Historical Society, 1973.

Wright, Gordon. France in Modern Times: 1760 to the Present. New York: Rand McNally and Co., 1960.

Wright, L. C. United States Policy Toward Egypt, 1830-1914. New York: Exposition-University Press, 1969.

Wriston, Merritt Henry. Executive Agents in American Foreign Relations. Baltimore: Johns Hopkins Press, 1929.

Articles:

Bryson, Thomas A. "William Brown Hodgson's Mission to Egypt, 1834," West Georgia College, Studies in the Social Sciences, XI (June 1972), 10-17.

Langley, Lester. "Jacksonian America and the Ottoman Empire," Muslim World, LXVIII (Jan.

1978), 46-56.

Mackall, Leonard L. "William Brown Hodgson," *Georgia Historical Quarterly*, XV (Dec. 1931), 324-345.

Nichols, Roy. "Diplomacy in Barbary," *Pennsylvania Magazine of History and Biography*, LXXIV (1950), 113-141.

Newspapers:

*National Intelligencer.*
*Niles Weekly Register.*
*Savannah Morning News.*
*Savannah Daily Georgian.*
*Savannah Republican.*
*United States Telegraph.*
*We the People.*

# INDEX

INDEX

A

Abd-er-rachman (Prince (Paul), 145
Abd er-Rahman, Sultan, 104
Abd es-Rahman, 40
Abderrahman, 110
Aberdeen, Lord, 153
Achmet Pacha, 92
Adams, John Quincy, 6, 8, 11, 12, 24, 25, 26, 27, 28, 36, 40
African Repository, 23, 40
Ahmed Bey, 125
"Albany Regency," 29, 36
Algiers, 3, 12, 13, 14, 15, 26, 35, 124, 143
American Colonization Society, 23, 145
American Oriental Society, 138, 139
American Philosophical Society, 15, 24, 133, 134
American System, 102, 110
Andrews, W. W., 126
Angelina, 58

Ascaroglou, 55, 56, 65, 73, 74, 77
Axson, Rev. I. S. K., 158

B

Balloon, 12, 13
Bainbridge, Captain William, 42
Ballard, Commo. Henry, 113, 114, 115
Barbars, 140
Barbary pirates, 3, 4, 11, 143
Barclay, Anthony, 153, 156
Baring Brothers, 73
Barnes, William, 25
Barron, Capt. James, 115
Bartlett, Edwin, 112-114
Bartow, Francis S., 155
Beled es-Sudan, 135
Ben-Ali (see Bu Allah), 141, 143, 145
Benton, Thomas Hart, 38, 123
Berber dialect, 15, 18-21, 139, 141
Berrien, John Macpherson, 149, 155
Biddle, Captain James, 43,

205

62, 115
Blair, Francis, 39
Boghos Bey, 90, 91, 94, 96
Bozo, Signore Antonio, 125
Brent, Daniel, 12, 16, 30
British and Foreign Bible Society, 23, 40
British Museum, 39
*British Queen*, 117
Brown, George F., 31, 61, 69
Brown, John Porter, 59, 61, 63, 81, 154
Bu Allah (see Ben-Ali), 141
Buchanan, James, 153

C

Calhoun, John C., 38, 39, 102, 157
Campbell, Colonel, 94
Campou Aghlan, 67, 68
Capudan Pacha, 52, 54, 59, 78
Carnahan, Rev. James, 7, 57
Cheves, Langdon, 152
Churchill, Bunker & Co., 78
Churchill, William N., 62, 73, 79
Civil War, 147, 156, 158
Clay, Henry, 12, 16, 17, 18, 25, 26, 28, 30, 38, 58, 102
Cockburn, Admiral, 143
Cohen, M. S., 68

Compromise of 1850, 151
Compromise Tariff of 1833, 101
Confederation of Peru and Bolivia, 110, 112, 114, 116
Constantinople, description of, 52
Constitution, U.S.S., 102, 104
consular service, 5, 62, 74, 75, 81, 129, 161
Cook, Daniel Pope, 8
Countess of Mulgrave, 110
Couper, James Hamilton, 135, 140, 141, 142, 150

D

D'Avezac, M., 134, 140, 144
Decatur, Stephen, 11, 124, 143
Delaware, U.S.S., 50, 80
Dickerson, Mahlon, 74
*Dolorita*, 111
*Dred Scott v. Sanford*, 152
DuHamel, Colonel, 94
Duponceau, Peter A., 15, 18, 19, 20, 21, 22, 24, 28, 29, 37, 39, 57, 110

E

Eckford, Henry, 44, 51, 52, 54, 76, 77, 78
Egypt,
    trade & international status, 90-96; relation to Ottoman Empire, 94; jurisprudence, 95; and Muhammad Ali, 97-98
Elliott, Capt. Jesse D., 62

Index    207

Encyclopedia Americana, 137
Enterprise, U.S.S., 112
Essex, U.S.S., 50
Ethnological Society of New York, 139, 144
Evans, Dr., 112
extraterritoriality, 77, 95

F

Falmouth, U.S.S., 112, 113, 114
Fellata (see Foulah), 136
Filani (see Foulah), 136
Finnie, David H., 51, 56, 91
Force, Peter, 13, 14, 15, 39, 97
Forsyth, John, 38, 81, 89, 92, 102, 106, 107, 108, 110, 112, 114, 116, 117, 123
Forsyth, Mrs. John, 38
Foulahs, 22, 136, 137, 140, 141, 144, 145, 146
France, 26, 103, 123-24
Franklin, Benjamin, 139
Fraser, Major, 23
Frederick William IV, 117
French Geographical Society, 142
Ful (see Foulahs), 136
Fulani (see Foulahs), 137, 138, 140
Fulbe (see Foulahs), 136

G

Gadsby's Hotel, 37
Gaspary, Guiseppe, 124
Gale, W. R. B., 126
Gallatin, Albert, 139
Georgia Historical Society, 147, 149, 150, 162
Gibbons, Sally, 127
Glendy, Captain, 115
Gliddon, George R., 91
Gliddon, John, 90, 91, 96, 97
Golden Isles of Georgia, 141
Goodell, Rev. William, 61, 62
"Gospels Written in the Negro Patois of English with Arabic Characters by a Mandingo Slave," 144
Great Britain, 103, 124
Green, Duff, 24, 39
Greenough, W. W., 138
Gurley, R. R., 40

H

Habersham, Dr. J. C., 150
Habersham, Robert, 155
Habib Effendi, 91
Haley, Alex, 143
Halim Effendi, 61
Hall, Luella, 105, 108
Hamet, 19, 23
Hamilton, James A., 30, 44
Hammond, James H., 151, 152, 153, 154, 155
Hanover, 117
Harrison, William Henry, 117, 118

Hawkins, Benjamin, 150
Hayne-Webster Debate, 39
Heap, Samuel D., Jr.,
    74, 121, 122, 125,
    126
Henrietta, 111
Hodgson Hall, 162
Hodgson, Joseph, 6, 7
Hodgson, Margaret T.,
    162
Hodgson, Rebecca, 6
Hodgson, Robert, 7
Hodgson, Very Rev.
    Robert, 128
Hodgson, William Brown,
    birth, 6; education,
    7; teaching, 7;
    Princeton confers de-
    gree on, 7; position
    at Department of
    State, 8; John
    McLean's patronage,
    8, 27, 39; posted to
    Algiers, 11; apti-
    tude for language
    study, 11, 12; at
    Gibraltar, 13; per-
    sonality traits of,
    14; Shaler's views on,
    14, 17, 21, 24; meets
    Algerian Minister of
    Marine, 14; studies
    Arabic, 15, 19; study
    of Lingua Franca, 16;
    Charge d'Affaires at
    Algiers, 18; study of
    Turkish, 17; study of
    Persian, 18; study of
    modern Greek, 18;
    study of Berber, 19;
    corresponds with Pe-
    ter S. Duponceau, 19;
    Hamet assists, 19; study of
    Foulahs, 22; interest in
    Sudan, 23; interest in Am-
    erican Colonization Socie-
    ty, 23; study of philology,
    23; translates Four Gos-
    pels into Berber, 23; and
    American Philosophical Soc-
    iety, 24; elected to Royal
    Asiatic Society, 24, 39;
    collects Oriental manu-
    scripts, 24; and Duff
    Green, 24; comments on
    French-Algerian dispute,
    25; poor health, 28; con-
    tact with Martin Van Buren,
    29; departed Algiers, 31;
    visits Duponceau, 35;
    visits Andrew Jackson, 35;
    visits Van Buren; Adams'
    views of, 36; translator at
    State Department, 37; cata-
    logue of manuscripts pub-
    lished, 39; elected to Am-
    erican Philosophical Socie-
    ty, 40; and American Colo-
    nization Society, 40; post-
    ed to Constantinople, 49;
    negotiates with Reis Effen-
    di, 54; Porter's early fav-
    or of, 54; knowledge of
    Turkish is questioned, 55;
    exchange of ratification,
    56; return to U.S., 58; ap-
    pointed dragoman, 59; re-
    turns to Constantinople, 59;
    negotiates with Turks, 60;
    faced with nepotism, 61;
    feud with Commo. Porter, 62;
    complains to Dept. of State,
    63; requests transfer, 64;
    Porter rebukes, 64; seeks

firman at Porte, 66; complains of nepotism, 68; removed as secretary of legation, 69; excluded from diplomatic society, 71; removed as dragoman, 72; question of his competence, 72; translation of Turkish treaty, 75; overstates his expertise, 75;Eckford episode, 76-79; and Dr. Lazzaro, 79; Porter presses charges against, 80; D. Porter assaults, 80; Forsyth not censure, 81; posted to Egypt, 86; mission to Egypt, 87-91; reports on Egypt, 90, 91, 92, 93, 94; departed Egypt, 91; wrote Sketch of Muhammad Ali, 97-98; returns to U.S., 101; posted to Morocco, 102; mission to Tangier, 102-109; visits Gibraltar, 104; usefulness at Tangier, 105-108; to Tetuan, 109; concern about employment, 109; presents Berber translation to Univ. of Va., 110; presents coins to A.P.S., 110; and Abderrahman, 110; publish in Journal of Royal Asiatic Society, 110; mission to Peru, 110-115; crosses Isthmus of Panama, 111; journey to LaPaz, 113; and Commo. Ballard, 114-115; and Captain Glendy, 115; returns from Peru, 116; observations on the Isthmus of Panama, 116; requests State Dept. post, 116; mission to Germany, 117; and Asiatic Society of Paris, 121; appointed consul at Tunis, 121; departs for Tunis, 124; presented to Bey of Tunis, 125; report on relations with Tunis, 126; leaves consular service, 126; departs Tunis, 126; decides to marry, 126; his anglophilia, 127; meets King and Queen of Naples, 127; resigns from consular service, 128; marries, 128; arrives at Savannah, 128; assessment of Berber research, 134; translation of Bible, 134; elected to Societe de Geographie, 134; and French colony in Algiers, 135; study of Africa, 135; interest in origin of African slaves, 135; ownership of slaves, 136; America's first Sudanist, 136; publishes "The Foulahs of Central Africa and the Slave Trade," 136; publishes in Encyclopedia Americana, 137; elected to American Oriental Society, 138; study of Georgia fossils, 138; spent summers in Newport and the autumn in New York, 139; publishes Notes on Northern Africa, the Sahara, and Soudan, 139; study of Tuarycks, 140, 142, 144;

## William Brown Hodgson

analysis of Berbers, 140; and James H. Couper, 140; geological and archaeological interests of, 142, 150; interest in Georgia history, 142; and New York Historical Society, 143; "Remarks on the Past History of Morocco, Algiers, and the Barbary Regencies," 143; reputed African scholar, 144; appointed commissioner to Paris Exposition of 1855, 144; receives French medal, 144; Ethnological Society of New York, 144, 146; "The Gospels Written in the Negro Patois,"144; discusses Dr. Barth, 146; scholarship in Civil War, 147; study of Sanscrit and Hebrew, 147; "The Science of Language: Sanscrit and Hebrew, the Two Written Primitive Languages Compared," 147; discussion on philology, 147-148; and the literary elite of Savannah, 149; joined Georgia Historical Society, 149; meeting at National Institute, 150; "Memoir on the Megatherium," 150; and Sir Charles Lyell, 150; edits Benjamin Hawkins' Sketch of the Creek Country, 150; and Georgia's colonial records, 150; and the slavery question, 151; his wife's plantations, 151; and James H. Hammond, 151; and Wilmot Proviso, 151; and Nashville Convention, 151; and Calhoun's dual system of govt., 151; and Compromise of 1850, 151; and secession, 152; and Oregon question, 153; Webster visits, 154; and wife's estate, 154-155; interest in plantations, 155; directorships, 155; attends Southern Commercial Convention, 155; interest in industry, 155; "Memoranda and the War," 156; and Union Army, 156; visits General Wm. T. Sherman, 157; penury, 157; on demise of slavery, 157; fire in Savannah, 158; death of, 158; funeral and burial, 158; summary of life, 161-62;

Hopeton Plantation, 140, 142, 150
Hunter, William P., 158
Hussein, Dey of Algiers, 15, 26, 31

I

Ibrahim, 65, 85, 89, 92

J

Jackson, Andrew, 8, 24, 28, 29, 30, 35, 36, 39, 40, 41, 42, 43, 49, 50, 51,

57, 58, 62, 101, 104, 109, 110
Jackson, Gen. Henry R., 158
John Adams, U.S.S., 44, 49, 51

### K

Kabayles, 15, 22, 142
Kaid Elabi Espaidi, 108
Key, Francis Scott, 7, 8
"King Andrew I", 102
Kirkland, Elizabeth, 62

### L

Lamartine, Baron, 70
Lane-Poole, Stanley, 54
Latham, R. G., 144
Lawrence, Alexander A., 154, 155
Lawton, Alexander, 155, 158
Lazzaro, Dr. Marino, 79
Lee, Major Henry, 24, 30, 31, 35, 36, 37, 51, 59
Lee, "Light Horse Harry," 30
Lee, Robert E., 30
Leib, James, 103, 104, 105, 106, 107, 108
Levant Company, 41
Lexington, U.S.S., 115
Lincoln, Abraham, 152
"Little Magician," 29, 35
Livingston, Edward, 51, 53, 54, 57, 58, 59, 60, 67, 68, 70, 72, 73, 74, 76, 86
Livingston, Mrs. Edward, 38
Long, David F., 61, 74
Louis Philippe, 135
Lyell, Sir Charles, 142, 150

### M

Medina, Jose Maria, 111
Mandingo, 144
Madison, James, 11
McKeever, Capt. Isaac, 112, 113
McLane, Louis, 73, 78, 81, 86, 87, 89
McLane, Mrs. Louis, 38
McLean, John, 8, 27, 28, 29, 36, 37, 39, 50, 87, 88, 102, 118, 121, 122, 123, 154
Mahmud, Sultan, 65, 66, 90
"March to the Sea," 156
Megatherium, 150
Meier, August, 136
"Memoir on the Megatherium and Other Extinct Quadrupeds of Georgia," 150
"Memoranda of the War," 156
Meninski, Mesgnient, 17
Miller, David Hunter, 55, 75
Missouri Compromise, 151
Monroe Doctrine, 4
Morgan, John Heath, 25
Morocco, 3, 11, 102, 108, 143
Mozabies, 22
Muhammad Ali, 65, 66, 85, 86, 87, 88, 89, 90, 92, 94, 96, 97
Murdock, George Peter, 137, 142

## N

Napoleon III, 144
Nashville Convention, 157
National Institution, 122, 126, 136, 138, 150
National Intelligencer, 7
National Journal, 39
Navoni, Nicholas, 53, 54, 55, 57, 58, 59, 73
Near Eastern Question, 88
"New South," 155
Newman, W.F., 134
New York Historical Society, 143
Nichols, Roy, 4
Nicholson, Capt. J.L., 80
Noah, Major, 123
North Carolina, U.S.S., 115
Notes of a Journey into the Interior of North Africa by Hadjii Ebn-ed-Din el Egh waati, 133
Notes on Northern Africa, the Sahara, and Sou-dan, 139, 144
nullification, 102

## O

Offley, David, 42, 43, 58
Omar (Moro), 145
Ontario, U.S.S., 13, 31
Oregon question, 153
Ottoman Turks, 14, 41

## P

Packenham, Richard, 153
Palmerston, Lord, 103, 105
Panic of 1837, 116
Paris Exposition of 1855, 144
Patterson, Commo. Daniel, 74, 79, 80, 85
Paullin, Charles O., 54, 156
Peul (see Foulahs), 136
Philadelphia, U.S.S., 50
Pickering, John, 138
Porter, Commo. David, 36, 44, 49, 50, 51, 52, 53, 54, 55, 56, 57, 58, 59, 60, 61, 62, 63, 64, 65, 66, 67, 68, 69, 70, 71, 72, 73, 74, 75, 76-78, 79-82, 85, 87, 88, 89, 91, 97, 118, 121, 122, 123
Porter, David Dixon, 56, 80
Porter, George, 60, 61, 62, 63
Prichard, Dr. James C., 134
Prince Job, 145
Prince Paul (see Abd-er-rachman), 145
Pullo (see Foulah), 136

## R

Reis Effendi, 49, 50, 53, 55, 60, 65, 66, 72
"Remarks on the Past History and Present Condition of Morocco, Algiers,

Index    213

and the Barbary Regencies," 143
Rhind, Charles, 43, 44
Richie, Thomas, 110
delRio, Juan Garcia, 114
Robert Fulton, 44
Rogers Act of 1924, 30
Romera, Col. Jose, 113, 114
rotation in office, 30
Royal Asiatic Society, 24, 39, 133
Rudwick, Elliott, 136

S

St. James Square, 156
Sali-bul-Ali, 140
Santa Cruz, Gen. Andrew, 112
Sapelo Island, 141
Savannah, 149, 156
Schulzinger, Robert, 5
"Science of Language: Sanscrit and Hebrew, the Two Written Primitive Languages Compared," 147
Screven, James P., 155
Screven, John, 158
Shaler, William, 11, 12, 13, 14, 15, 16, 17, 18, 19, 20, 21, 24, 25, 26, 28, 29, 30, 31, 35, 36, 37, 40, 64, 144
Sherman, General William T., 156, 157
Smithsonian Institution, 136
Societe de Geographie, 133, 140

Spalding, Thomas, 141, 143, 145
spoils system, 30
Stevens, William Bacon, 142, 150
Stevenson, Andrew, 57, 117
Stevenson, Mrs. Andrew, 38
Sublime Porte, 43, 52, 53, 60, 65, 67, 88, 94, 95
Sudan, 135, 136, 137, 141, 145
Sumner, George, 153

T

Taney, Roger B., 152
Tangier, 103, 104
Tattnall, Cdr. Joseiah, 115
Telfair, Edward, 127
Telfair family, 154, 155, 156, 157
Telfair, Margaret, 127
Telfair, Mary, 127
Tenedos, 59
Thiers, Louis, 105
Thornton, James E., 110, 112
Tom (see Sali-bul-Ali), 140, 142, 143
Toronto, 117
Toureg, 146, 147
Transactions of the American Philosophical Society, 24, 35, 133
Tripoli, 3, 15, 143
Tuarycks, 140, 142, 144, 146, 147
Tunis, 3, 15, 121, 122, 143
Turkey, 41, 77, 85
Turnbull, Archibald, 56, 65
Tyler, John, 121, 126, 128

## U

United States, U.S.S., 80
U.S. Department of State, 6, 8, 11, 25, 36, 40, 73, 75, 76, 81, 122, 123
United States Telegraph, 39

## V

Van Buren, Martin, 28, 29, 31, 35, 36, 37, 40, 41, 49, 50, 51, 57, 69, 74, 102, 116, 117
Vaughn, John, 39
Vitalle, Mr., 79
Vorhees, Capt., 52

## W

Wadreagans, 22
Waring, J. Fred, 149
Washington, D.C., description of, 37
Washington Globe, 39
Watterson, George, 7
Wayne, James M., 149
Webster, Daniel, 38, 102, 118, 121, 122, 125, 126, 128, 154
Wheaton, Henry, 117
Whig Party, 102
Wilmot Proviso, 151
Woodford, Major General Sir Alex, 104
Woodford, Lady, 104
Wurlegans, 23